THE RESTORATION OF THE
APOSTLES *and* *Prophets*

HÉCTOR TORRES

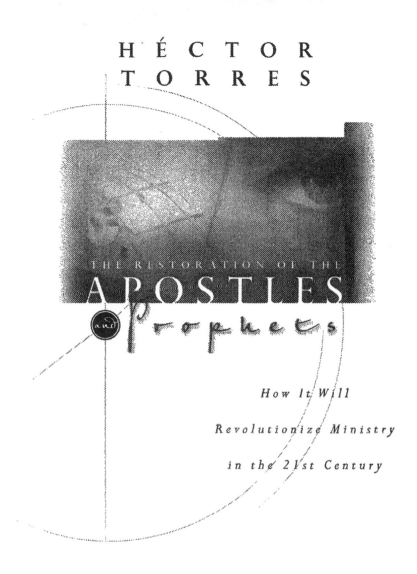

THE RESTORATION OF THE

APOSTLES *and* prophets

*How It Will
Revolutionize Ministry
in the 21st Century*

THOMAS NELSON PUBLISHERS
Nashville

Library of Congress Cataloging-in-Publication Data

Torres, Héctor, 1946–
    [Apóstoles y Profetas. English]
    The restoration of the Apostles and Prophets: and how it will revolutionize ministry in the 21st century/Héctor Torres.
    p. cm.
    ISBN 0-7852-4608-8
    1. Apostolate (Christian theology) 2. Prophecy—Christianity. 1. Title.

BV601.2 .T6713 2001
262'.1—dc21   00–053709

Printed in the United States of America
1 2 3 4 5 6 7 8 9 0 — 06 05 04 03 02 01

Table of Contents

Foreword

At the beginning of the twenty-first century, the Church finds itself in a privileged situation. It is evident that God has decided to do something amazing in the world today, allowing us to see abundant evangelistic fruit, while common saints are performing signs and wonders like those of the New Testament.

An element central to this situation in which the Church is living and of which we are witnesses is the restoration, after much, much time, of the offices of apostles and prophets. Héctor Torres sees this with complete clarity. He is one of the people who hears what the Spirit is saying to the churches. This book appears at precisely the right moment. *The Restoration of the Apostles and Prophets* is one of the first books on this important movement of God, and it is good. Héctor not only shares his own vision, but has succeeded in bringing together a team that represents the highest quality of thought today on this subject.

Because the recognition of the offices of apostle

and prophet is so new, I imagine that many readers of this book are going to feel a bit uncomfortable upon the start of this reading. It is to be expected, but in this foreword I want to describe the historical foundation upon which God is building today.

The historical roots of this new movement of God have to lie in the Protestant Reformation. The theology of the Reform remains strong due to our opinions of the authority of Scripture, the justification by faith and the priesthood of all the believers. Another key component is John Wesley's thoughts regarding personal sanctification. The modern missionary movement, begun two hundred years ago, has removed any doubt whatsoever about our role in spreading the gospel around the world.

In the twentieth century, the Pentecostal Movement has emphasized the third person of the Trinity, teaching us that the proclamation of the gospel ought to be accompanied by a supernatural power. In the 1950s, with the beginning of the ministry of Billy Graham, Oral Roberts, T. L. Osborne, Morris Cerullo, and many others, evangelism came to occupy the primary place. The decade of the sixties brought a new consciousness among Christians to aid the poor and oppressed. The great Global Prayer Movement was born in the 1970s. In the 1980s the gift and office of the prophet began to be recognized, and the gift and office of the apostle took relevance in the nineties.

It is odd that Christian leaders have not begun

to understand true church government until recently. The New Testament is full of revelations about the functions of apostles and prophets. In fact, they are the true foundation of the Church: "[The household of God] having been built on the foundation of the apostles and prophets, Jesus Christ Himself being the chief cornerstone" (Ephesians 2:20). Notwithstanding the past, it is exciting to be part of the generation that is now seen as the structure of the church as God originally designed it to be.

Upon reading *Apostles and Prophets* you will clearly see the profile that the Church is taking. You will be drinking of the river of God, and I assure you that when you finish, you yourself will be flowing within this divine river.

C. Peter Wagner, Chancellor
Wagner Leadership Institute

Preface

The great Christian movements of the past have served a vital purpose in their times to move the Church toward the restoration of all things. With the restoration of the ministerial gifts of the apostle, prophet, evangelist, pastor, and teacher of Ephesians 4, the body of Christ is beginning to reach maturity. Only when the office of apostle is restored will we be able to reach the fullness of Christ (Hebrews 3:1) within his people.

We live in a *kairos* time for humanity, a time of transition. Upon entering the twenty-first century, the Church should be restored in its fullness as has been the eternal purpose of God in fulfilling the mandate of the Great Commission and in making disciples of the nations for the Lord Jesus Christ. This period of transition has been called "postdenomenational" or "the new apostolic reform." This generation of apostles should show itself with power, not simply with eloquent words, if we desire to see productivity that transforms the entire world. When thousands of apostles begin to stand up in their ministry, the Church will become free to effectively disciple nations that are open to receiving the Lordship of Christ.

The harvest cannot be reaped without this fundamental role. We are seeing the Father raise a new generation of apostles and apostolic people who are taking their place in the world, offering a valuable contribution to the work of God. This requires a fresh anointing and people desirous of embracing the new, while holding fast to the fundamentals of yesterday. This must require people of anointing and integrity to mark time toward the gathering of cities and nations as the Church of the first century did, and in this way establishing the kingdom of Christ here on earth.

Dr. Stan DeKoven, President
Vision International University
Ramonita, California

Introduction

Now the LORD had said to Abram:
"Get out of your country,
From your kindred
And from your father's house,
To a land that I will show you.
I will make you a great nation;
I will bless you
And make your name great;
And you shall be a blessing.
I will bless those who bless you,
And I will curse him who curses you;
And in you all the families of the earth shall be blessed."

Genesis 12:1–3

When God wants to do something new in our lives, he generally asks from us something that requires the abandonment of that which is known, comfortable, and to which we are emotionally and spiritually attached. We should observe that the Bible tells us that Jehovah "had said." That is to say that in the past God had been speaking to Abram about the changes he desired to make so that he would be blessed.

One of the most difficult things for individuals to do is to abandon or leave the place they feel comfortable, where they feel secure, that familiar place. Because of this, many times, though God tells us something, we delay in obeying, and many times we need someone to push us or force us to take the initial steps toward making these changes. In the case of Abram, God used his father, Terah, to take Abram from the place where he was tarrying. We are to understand that although God had told Abram to abandon everything and he would be blessed, he never took the necessary steps until his father did it for him.

And Terah took his son Abram and his grandson Lot, the son of Haran, and his daughter-in-law Sarai, his son Abram's wife, and they went out with them from Ur of the Chaldeans to go to the land of Canaan; and they came to Haran and dwelt there. So the days of Terah were two hundred and five years, and Terah died in Haran. Genesis 11:31–32

While many of us desire for God to speak to us and reveal his plans for our life, we are not always interested in making changes or adjustments to our lives. Biblically, this is impossible. When God speaks to his servants in the Bible about his plans and purposes, he always demands of them changes and adjustments in their lives and in their plans in order to conform them to his own. Being prepared to adjust our life, our beliefs, our plans, and even the place where we live is a critical point in being able to experience the purpose of God in our lives.

God is always doing something new and different for the progress of His kingdom. All progress brings changes. All growth produces changes, and all changes bring new challenges. It is very fitting to say that not all change represents progress, but without change there can be no progress.

I am not writing this book to impress anyone. I do hope that through its content you can have a new and fresh experience with God. To be able to proceed with God we have to be ready to change the things that have ceased to be effective and seek the new things God wants to do.

If we truly desire to see a spiritual awakening, to experience a revival, to uncover ways to transform our communities, perhaps we must admit that the methods and strategies that we have been using have not been effective, that they have not brought the desired results that are necessary to bring changes. To see new things we have to engage in new things.

God told Abram to leave his land, his kinsmen, and his father's house. If Abram was prepared to obey God's demands, he would receive great and marvelous blessings.

In the following pages, allow God to speak to you; listen with his Spirit; open your heart; do not criticize; be inclined to open your ears and your heart. For some the changes will be radical, for others they will only be small adjustments, and for even others it will be a confirmation to continue on the path they are following.

Just as Abraham "believed God, and it was accounted to him for righteousness." Therefore know that only those who are of faith are sons of Abraham. And the Scripture, foreseeing that God would justify the nations by faith, preached the gospel to Abraham beforehand, saying, "In you all the nations shall be blessed." So then those who are of faith are blessed with believing Abraham. Galatians 3:6–9

God essentially is telling him, "If you listen and obey, I will bless you." We cannot put new wine in old wineskins, because they will explode, and the new wine will be lost. In the same way, we cannot remain in the past if we desire to reach the future. Luke tells us Stephen's words before the Jewish council regarding Abraham's calling, saying:

And he said, "Men and brethren and fathers, listen: The God of glory appeared to our father Abraham when he was in Mesopotamia, before he dwelt in Haran, and said to him, 'Get out of your country and from your relatives, and come to a land that I will show you.' Then he came out of the land of the Chaldeans and dwelt in Haran. And from there, when his father was dead, He moved him to this land in which you now dwell. And God gave him no inheritance in it, not even enough to set his foot on. But even when Abraham had no child, He promised to give it to him for a possession, and to his descendants after him." Acts 7:2-5

God has a plan for each generation, and God is providing us with technological, economical, and spiritual advances for the new millennium. The church of the twenty-first century cannot remain in a twentieth century mindset, just as the twentieth century Church did not remain in the confines of the nineteenth century.

That the blessing of Abraham might come upon the Gentiles in Christ Jesus, that we might receive the promise of the Spirit through faith. Galatians 3:14

God's challenge to us is to abandon our place of comfort and extend our vision, to rise to a new level of faith in order to see new manifestations of the glory of God. God desires that we live from faith to faith and from glory to glory. To God it is not important what we know, but that we have a spirit that is teachable and open to hearing Him.

If we want to be synchronized with God, we have to be obedient and teachable. This is going to require that we be prepared to pay the price that God demands of us.

In Matthew 1:18-25 the angel of the Lord reveals to Joseph God's plans for sending the promised Messiah. The words of the angel challenge all aspects of life for this man of God. As he was betrothed to Mary, he had to accept the fact that his fiancé was pregnant with a baby conceived miraculously. He was to go against the Jewish traditions and the gossip of his peers (Matthew 1:18–21) and to obey God (Matthew 1:24–25).

Afterward, Herod proposed to massacre children under the age of two, and the angel of the Lord appeared anew to Joseph in his dreams to order him to take the child and his mother to Egypt and to remain there until Herod's death. These changes, certainly radical, demanded the obedience to abandon everything in order that the purposes of God for all of humanity succeed. When we are open to these things, we will discover our divine destiny.

Some of the adjustments or changes of paradigm that God requires of us can be in different areas.

- *In our circumstances (work, finances, home)*

- *In our relationships (prejudices, methods, business)*

- *In our predispositions or doctrines (in family, church, work, tradition, etc.)*

- *In our actions (praying, giving, serving, loving, living, etc.)*

- *In our beliefs (about God, his purposes, his ways, and our relationship with Him)*

I understand that some parts of this book will be controversial, but I should take the risk that God demands if I desire to share in seeing a change in the Church. Changes always bring hostile repercussions on the part of the established order. Jesus

Christ attacked the errors and hypocrisy of the Pharisees and Sadducees and was prepared to die for the cause of the reform. Martin Luther and other patriarchs of the Protestant Reformation refuted the doctrinal errors of the Church as their objective was to preach and teach the truth no matter the cost.

By the grace of God, I have been put in a strategic place for the Church in recent times. God has given us the privilege of working with great servants of God in Latin America, in the United States, and around the world. Consequently, I have been able to observe from up close the movement of the Holy Spirit and sit down at the table of those who are in the vanguard of the New Apostolic Reformation.

My fervent desire is that all those who are open to the fresh movement of the Spirit could receive a confirmation of what is happening, could have some concerns clarified, and could receive a basic and fundamental instruction for God's proceeding in their lives and ministries.

The apostle John, inspired by the Holy Spirit, writes to the Saints:

These things I have written to you who believe in the name of the Son of God, that you may know that you have eternal life, and that you may continue to believe in the name of the Son of God. I John 5:13

Likewise, the apostle Luke declares that the purpose of writing the gospel was to present in order all the things that Jesus began to do and teach

(Acts 1:1) in such a way that Theophilus would know the historical evidences of the teachings he had received (1:4). Without claiming the same level of inspiration as the aforementioned apostles, nor having the same authority as them, my desire is to share the origin of this new apostolic and prophetic movement and give a chronological telling of the events that surround it.

My prayer is that the reader be informed, established, and, it goes without saying, blessed by the content of this book. The participants in the content of this book are men highly recognized for their international ministries. They are apostles and prophets who are on the vanguard of the new apostolic reformation.

1

The Restoration of All Things

*Repent therefore and be converted, that your sins may be blotted out, so that times of refreshing may come from the presence of the Lord, and that He may send Jesus Christ, who was preached to you before, whom heaven must receive until the times of **restoration of all things,** which God has spoken by the mouth of all His holy prophets since the world began.*   Acts 3:19–21

In the last days, we will live in moments of refreshment—a period of refreshing revival as a result of a genuine repentance, and a precursor to the return of the Lord Jesus Christ, according to what the apostle Peter declares. For this to occur, there is one condition, one necessary occurrence: the *restoration of all things.* The word restoration signifies returning something or someone to the state in which they once were. If something is restored, it is because it has deteriorated from its original condition or that it has simply been neglected to the point of its destruction. Restoration is then, the process of correcting a condition through a process of change.

1

Scripture shows us that when God restores, things not only return to their original condition, but the restored work surpasses the original. For example, in Mosaic law, if someone was found guilty of theft, that person was required to return four or five times the value of what was stolen. When God restored to Job that which Satan had robbed from him, he blessed him even more abundantly and gave him double of that which he had lost. The prophet Joel, to whom the apostle Peter refers, declared that the later outpouring would be greater than the first. When God restores, he multiplies, and because of this, the church of the end times is being restored in a way more powerful and more glorious than the first.

Be glad then, you children of Zion,
And rejoice in the LORD your God;
For He has given you the former rain faithfully,
And He will cause the rain to come down for you—
The former rain,
And the latter rain in the first month.
The threshing floors shall be full of wheat,
And the vats shall overflow with new wine and oil.
So I will restore to you the years that the swarming
 locust has eaten,
The crawling locust,
The consuming locust,
And the chewing locust,
My great army which I sent among you.
You shall eat in plenty and be satisfied,

And praise the name of the LORD your God,
Who has dealt wondrously with you;
And My people shall never be put to shame.

Joel 2:23–26

The verb *restore* is the same word as return or re-establish. The prophet Isaiah, describing the people of God as "robbed and plundered, snared, hidden, and prey" (Isaiah 42:22), seems to be talking of the spiritual condition of today's church. This description concludes with a mandate from the celestial throne, an order from the commander of the heavenly armies: *Restore.*

To give this order implies that God seeks our collaboration to bring about the purposes that he desires to carry out. The sovereign God chooses to involve us in his purposes and plans! We are *God's fellow workers* (I Corinthians 3:9), and we have been called to continue with the work that Jesus Christ began both to do and to teach (Acts 1:1).

Throughout history, the Lord has been restoring to his Church *all* that which the enemy has robbed through deceits and false philosophies based on traditions of man and not on Christ.

The ministry of Jesus Christ appeared on the scene in a time for Israel in which God had not spoken to his people in more than four hundred years. The nation of God had sold itself to the government of Rome. It decided to throw aside the precepts and teachings of the prophets in order to avoid confrontation and so retain control over the people of Israel. Then Jesus appears. He presents himself as a messenger from God, an apostle, an ambassador of the throne of heaven; and he arrives commissioned with power and authority to confront, judge, and reform the house of God.

The prophet Haggai had declared that the glory of God's latter temple would be greater than the former. To fulfill the prophecy, Jesus manifested himself to restore that which the people had lost. These are the things that the apostolic ministry of Christ came to restore:

- *Sound doctrine*

- *The power and authority of God*

- *The government or judgment of his people*

- *A fresh, new revelation of the plans and purposes of God*

- *A spiritual awakening or revival*

Disciples, apostles, and prophets

In the first section of Matthew 10, observe that Jesus calls his men "disciples," but once he gives them authority, he calls them "apostles." That is, they were commissioned with power and authority (vs. 2), and now he sends them out as ambassadors, his representatives before the Jewish people. Jesus

4

specifically ordered them *not to enter* the cities of the Samaritans. It was necessary that the gospel of the kingdom be delivered first to the Jews. As ambassadors of Jesus, the Apostles were commissioned with a limited amount of delegated power and authority. The outpouring of the Holy Spirit on the day of Pentecost removed these limitations and gave them the anointing to be representatives of Christ throughout the entire world.

Upon returning to heaven, Jesus Christ left with His people the dynamic and creative power of the Holy Spirit. Additionally, He gave ministerial gifts so that His Church would spread throughout the world and establish the kingdom of God here on earth by saving the lost and destroying the works of the enemy. This what is known as the Great Commission.

> *And He Himself gave some of them to be apostles, some prophets, some evangelists, and some pastors and teachers, for the equipping of the saints for the work of ministry, for the edifying of the body of Christ, till we all come to the unity of the faith and the knowledge of the Son of God, to a perfect man, to the measure of the stature of the fullness of Christ.* Ephesians 4:11–13

The purpose of God in giving ministerial gifts is to perfect—to prepare, train, equip, or enable the body of Christ—so that we all may come to the fullness of Christ and unity of the faith.

For the building of His Church, God established

that the foundation be laid upon the apostles and prophets. To these He charged the coordination of the government and administration of the Church. The prophets give the instructions that proceed from God and the apostles administer their execution.

Having been built on the foundation of the apostles and prophets, Jesus Christ Himself being the chief cornerstone, in whom the whole building, being joined together, grows into a holy temple in the Lord, in whom you also are being built together for a habitation of God in the Spirit. Ephesians 2:20–22

God uses the apostles and prophets to receive—through the Holy Spirit—the revelation of what is hidden. He gives this revelation to them that they may proclaim it to his people and institute the changes that this new revelation requires.

The apostle Paul writes that it was given to him to understand the mystery of the Church as the body of Christ, of which He is the head, and we are the body.

How that by revelation He made known to me the mystery (as I wrote before in a few words, by which when you read, you may understand my knowledge in the mystery of Christ), which in other ages was not made known to the sons of men, as it has now been revealed by the Spirit to His holy apostles and prophets: that the Gentiles should be fellow heirs, of the same body, and partakers of His promise in Christ through the gospel. Ephesians 3:3–6

The Church in the first years

During the first five hundred years of the Church, false doctrines infiltrated it, trying to slowly drown and destroy it. Little by little, these erroneous doctrines were robbing the Church of the spiritual gifts and ministries that God had given to it. The leadership of the Church fell into apostasy and forsook its calling, entered into an infernal relationship with the Roman government, and departed from the holy doctrine, throwing aside the precepts of the faith handed down by the Church fathers. The apostle Paul refers to these as shipwrecks concerning the faith (I Timothy 1:1–19); men of corrupt minds, disapproved concerning the faith (II Timothy 3:3–8).

Dr. Pablo Deiros, director of the Baptist Theological Seminary in Buenos Aires, Argentina, describes in his wonderful book *The Work of the Holy Spirit in History (La acción del Espíritu Santo en la historia,* Caribe-Betania, 1998) how with the passing of the years, the manifestations of the Holy Spirit were being removed from the Church. Deiros explains that upon instituting the doctrine of cessationism, the Church eliminated from its use the ministries of the apostle, then of the prophet, the evangelist, and the teacher. This process resulted in the establishment of an ecclesiastical hierarchy very different from that established by Christ and by the Bible.

Men's doctrines began to have more authority than the Word of God. Soon the government of the

Church was altered, and the manifestations of the Holy Spirit were prohibited and could not be practiced nor taught. In this way a religious governing body was formed that removed the glory of God from its midst, turning into an *ichabod* church, that is to say, a church without life. Nonetheless, God has *always* kept a faithful remnant, that through the years and in God's proper time *(kairos)* has stood up to bring changes and reforms that conform to the Word of God and its doctrines.

When God restores something that the Church has lost, the end result is a spiritual awakening that leads to great revival. Generally speaking, these are so powerful that they transform religious entities, confront the established social order and renew the spiritual life of thousands of people.

Thus, God raised up a man named Martin Luther and gave him the revelation of justification through grace by faith and not through works. Luther stood up to confront the ecclesiastical authorities and bring reforms to many false doctrines. The Christian Church today walks by this revelation, which had been lost and was only recognized by a small remnant. God needed an apostolic anointing to give understanding to the church of Luther's generation.

The Protestant Reformation of the sixteenth century brought about a spiritual revival that shook the entire world. The changes were evident in entire communities that were transformed by the power of this new revelation of the grace of God. Church history teaches us that in the year 1517, God began to restore lost truths. This was a process of radical changes instituted by the Holy Spirit to rescue, correct, and strengthen his Church.

In his book, *Apostles, Prophets and the Coming Moves of God,* Dr. Bill Hamon describes the process of restoration of truths lost by the Church throughout the years.

Restoration

Year	Movement	Major Truth Restored
1517	Protestant	Salvation by grace through faith (Ephesians 2:8–9).
1600	Evangelical	Water baptism, separation of Church and state.
1700	Holiness	Sanctification, the Church set apart from the world.
1800	Faith Healing	Divine healing for the physical body, healing in the atonement.
1900	Pentecostal	Holy Spirit baptism with speaking in tongues; gifts of the Holy Spirit.
1950	Latter Rain	Prophetic presbytery, singing praises and melodious worship.

Restoration—*cont'd*

Year	Movement	Major Truth Restored
1950	Deliverance	Evangelist ministry and mass evangelism Evangelism reactivated.
1960	Charismatic	Renewal of all restored truth to all past movement churches. Pastors were restored to being sovereign head of their local churches.
1970	Faith	Faith confessions, prosperity and victorious attitude and life. Teacher ministry reestablished as a major fivefold minister.
1980	Prophetic	Prophetic, activating gifts, warfare praise, prophets to nations. Prophet ministry was restored and a company of prophets brought forth.
1990	Apostolic	Miraculous signs and wonders, apostolic ministry, and unity, great harvest of souls, Apostle ministry being restored to bring divine order and structure, finalize restoration of fivefold ministers.

How to understand the process of change

Dr. Bill Hamon, in his book *Prophets and the Prophetic Movement* writes:

> However, we must understand the process that every restoration movement has gone through since the beginning of Church restoration. The leaders and people that have been used by God to restore the biblical foundations and the spiritual experiences are initially rejected, persecuted and despised by the mainstream Christian denominations and by groups linked to previous movements of God. These people are seen as very controversial within the Church; they are accused of being fanatics, heretics, false prophets and teachers, and even cult leaders. (see Matt. 23:29–39)
>
> When truth is being restored in the Church, usually there is a sudden swing to the opposite side, then it swings back to where it started. Finally, it rests upon a balanced message, like the pendulum of an old grandfather's clock, between two extremes. Those who are trapped between those extremes become sectarian in their dogmas from a doctrinal and practical standpoint. From there spring up exclusive groups that drift away from the rest of the Body of Christ. Then, there are those who drift away from the extremes to keep an adequate biblical balance, and ultimately become a part of the restoring movement of God.[1]

1 Dr. Bill Hamon, *Prophets and the Prophetic Movement*, (Destiny Image. 1990), p. 124.

The most bitter enemies of God's reforms have usually been the religious systems, who find themselves confronted with truths that put their "power" at risk and threaten the control they exercise. During the time of Christ, they were the Pharisees and Sadducees. During the Protestant Reformation, it was the Catholic hierarchy. During the spiritual awakening to divine healing brought to light by an apostle named Alexander Dowie, the opposition came from the Church and from the mass media that incited the authorities to quiet this "charlatan."

The same thing happened during the revelation of the movement of the Holy Spirit in Azusa, California, when the Church rejected what was new and called it a "movement of the devil." Presently, in many areas of the world there still exists a strong rejection of the faith and prosperity movement. In many religious circles the topic of spiritual warfare is looked upon with mistrust, the same is true with all that concerns the apostolic and prophetic movements.

Nonetheless, when God brings reform, it is *He* who defends His cause against *all* the opposition that may exist. When the religious system of Babylon and its false teachers were exposed, God judged in favor of His apostles and prophets.

Rejoice over her, O heaven, and you holy apostles and prophets, for God has avenged you on her!
Revelation 18:20

Jesus Christ began His ministry on earth commissioning twelve men as apostles and in order to bring reform to the nation of Israel. Apostles open the way for the moves of God. They were the first to be established and the first to be eliminated by the apostate church, but in the words of Christ: *The first will be last and the last first* (Matthew 19:30).

As we have seen, the Church was eliminating that which God had set as a systematic order for His Church.

And God has appointed these in the church: first apostles, second prophets, third teachers, after that miracles, then gifts of healings, helps, administrations, varieties of tongues. I Corinthians 12:28

In the same manner, the restoration of all things has also occurred in a systematic order, from the last to the first and from the first to the last. This century has brought great blessings to the Church, and as we get closer to the Lord's return, the restoration of that which was lost has been more accelerated.

At the beginning of the century—and through a black apostle named William J. Seymour—God poured out a revival in Azusa, California, which rapidly spread through the whole world. It was the restoration of speaking in tongues, a fresh breeze of Pentecost that spread throughout the world and radically changed the structure of the Evangelical Church.

In the 1930s, 40s, and 50s, the ministries of healing and miracles were reestablished, thanks to the anointing of different evangelists. Men like Oral Roberts, John G. Lake, Smith Wigglesworth, and women such as Aimee Sample Mcpherson and Kathryn Kuhlman were pioneers of this time.

In the 1970s, a fresh anointing came over the ministry of the gift of teaching. The message of faith, prosperity, identification with Christ, and the restoration of Zion was proclaimed and taught by these teachers. Men such as Ken Copeland, Derek Prince, Bob Munford, John Osteen, Chuck Smith, John Wimber, and many more participated in this awakening.

During the 1980s, God raised up the ministry of the prophet. Prophets began prophesying to individuals. Later, God raised up prophets to carry a message to the nations, and most recently he raised them up for the cities. Men like Bill Hamon, Paul Caine, Mike Bickle, John Sandford, Rick Joyner, Victor and Eduardo Lorenzo, and women like Cindy Jacobs, Barbara Yoder, Jill Griffith, Paula Sanford, Marfa Cabrera, and many more revived this ministry around the world.

In the 1990s, a restoration of the apostolic ministry began, with the purpose of the Church entering the new millennium in the fullness of Christ, having the five ministries: apostle, prophet, evangelist, pastor, and teacher. Today we have apostles such as Dr. David Chou, Dr. C. Peter Wagner, Dr. Kingsley Fletcher, John Kelly, Cesar Castellanos, John Eckhardt, Omar Cabrera, Randy McMillan, Luciano Padilla, Ernesto Alonzo, Victor Ricardo, Nahum Rosario, Harold Caballeros, and many more.

According to Dr. C. Peter Wagner, post-denominational affiliations are springing forth around the world which are coming together for what has been called the New Apostolic Reformation. This movement is generating the most radical changes in church government since the sixteenth century.

There is no doubt that God is bringing about these changes to the Church to restructure its government and to reveal new strategies. In order to accomplish His objective of establishing the kingdom of heaven here on earth, God is restoring all the truths that had been lost. Those who refuse to accept this movement of the Spirit, with His new and marvelous strategies, in the end will cease to produce fruit and will disappear.

It is necessary for the Church to continue in this process of change and restoration so that it can rise up and accomplish its mission of revolutionizing the world. In the next chapter we will discuss in more detail the history of the restoration movements and their extremes.

2

The History of Restoration

"The glory of this latter temple shall be greater than the former," says the LORD of hosts. "And in this place I will give peace," says the LORD of hosts.   Haggai 2:9

For the LORD will restore the excellence of Jacob
Like the excellence of Israel,
For the emptiers have emptied them out
And ruined their vine branches.   Nahum 2:2

For I will give you a mouth and wisdom which all your adversaries will not be able to contradict or resist.
                                        Luke 21:15

Since the beginning of creation, every time God does a new work, the enemy opposes the divine plans and purposes through the actions of man. In fact, when we speak of restoration, we must go back to the creation of man. God created man and placed him in the middle of the garden to tend and keep it (Genesis 2:15). To bring about this work, He gave man *dominion* over all things and commissioned him to be fruitful and multiply and to fill the earth, subdue it, and have control over it. Then along came the enemy, and man fell. As a consequence of this fall, man lost the authority and dominion he had been given. At that moment, Jehovah declared the beginning of restoration with the promise of a Redeemer who would come through the seed of woman. "This first messianic promise is one of the most succinct asseverations of the gospel that we can find."[1]

Through His life, death, and resurrection, Jesus Christ broke the power of darkness, He canceled and erased the sin of man, and most importantly, reconciled us to the original plan. The curse was broken—nailed on the cross—hallelujah!

So Jesus once again granted authority and power to man to complete the work He had begun. Now the mission is to establish the kingdom of God here on earth, which is why He gives us the ministry of reconciliation (II Corinthians 5:18). To establish His Church, He commissioned it with *power* and so, that first Church became a glorious and victorious force.

Gradually, and with the passing of years, the Church abandoned the apostles' doctrine and became lost in traditions and philosophies of man. Supernatural powers, manifestations of the Holy Spirit, the church government, soundness, prosperity—in short, the Church victorious entered into a

1 *The Spirit Filled Life Bible*, (Thomas Nelson Publishers, 1991).

process of decadence. The apostle Paul called it apostasy and the mystery of lawlessness (II Thessalonians 2:3–7); they were doctrines of demons and deceiving spirits.

> *Now the Spirit expressly says that in latter times some will depart from the faith, giving heed to deceiving spirits and doctrines of demons.*   I Timothy 4:1

Historians have called this period the Middle Ages (Matthew 24, II Thessalonians 3:10–12, II Peter 3:15–17). The apostle Peter spoke prophetically then, declaring that in the latter days would come times of refreshment (Acts 3:19) and of the *restoration of all things* (vs. 21).

More than a thousand years have passed, and just as God raised up Moses to give the law to His people and sent down Christ to destroy the works of evil and establish His Church, He raised up His servant Martin Luther to begin the process of the restoration of all the things that the Church had lost.

We have to understand that Luther was a Roman Catholic priest and that to be Christian in that age was to hold to the Orthodox Church and the Roman Church. As in *all* times of restoration, the most fierce opposition came from the religious leaders of the established order, who quickly called those who tried to bring about change false prophets, heretics, false teachers, fanatics, and leaders of sects. This has been repeated throughout history: the

Pharisees and Sadducees did this to Jesus and later with his disciples; the idolaters of Ephesus to Paul and His disciples; and the Roman leaders to the faithful Christians, to name a few.

We should say with sadness that in the last five hundred years of Protestant Christendom, when God does something new, the strongest opposition *always* comes from those who previously have enjoyed a visitation from God.

The pendulum of truth

Many times, when a truth is restored to the Church, those who participated in the previous movement of God place themselves in positions which are completely extreme and which bring about abuses and seek to discredit the fresh movement of the Spirit. Thanks be to God that with the passing of time, the majority return to a biblical-doctrinal balance that permits that truth to begin to be accepted by those who are open to the direction of the Holy Spirit. Those who cling to the extremes, to the right or the left, become exclusive groups that set themselves apart from the rest of the body of Christ.

> *The fact remains that there will always be those who are biblically uneducated and who never become birthed in the present truth. There will always be those who are emotionally unstable and spiritually immature who can not handle the truth, so they start doing weird things*

that are out of order concerning the present truth. And there will always be charlatans, false ministers and those who are wrongly motivated, looking for an opportunity to promote themselves and to profit from the movement.[1]

Errors and extremes

The doctrinal message of the fifteenth century Church was based on works, indulgences, and rituals that gave way to a life of sin and lasciviousness. Expiation could be bought from the ecclesiastical leaders with money or with favors. With the revelation of the message of salvation by faith and not by works, the doctrine of justification rose to theological extremes, like Calvinism and Armenianism.

In the first case, Calvinism defends individual predestination of the saints, apart from free will. Armenianism, on the other hand, postulates a salvation for all who receive Christ as Savior, but this salvation can be lost, and one can fall from the grace of God. In this case, salvation is temporal and is based on a life of complete holiness. Both doctrines still prevail in many areas of Christianity due to ignorance of the Word, that affirms a predestination for the Church as a whole—the body of Christ—and an eternal salvation for all who are born again, and thus become a part of the Church.

1 Dr. Bill Hamon, *Prophets and the Prophetic Movement*, (Destiny Image Publishers), 1990, p. 126.

The process of the restoration of the ministry offices has also been gradual. Among the callings restored to the Church, we find the following: "The role of the pastor was restored during the Protestant Reformation in the sixteenth century, replacing the clerical office of priest that had overtaken the Church. The role of evangelist had been virtually ignored until the times of Charles Finney in the nineteenth century."[1]

Approximately one hundred years later, the Church understood the revelation of baptism by immersion. Even today we see extremes in relation to the correct "baptismal formula." On one side, infant baptism—still practiced by various Christian denominations—and on the other, those who give little or no importance to water baptism. Some demand that baptism be in the name of the Father, the Son, and the Holy Spirit (Matthew 28:19). Others say that it should be only in the name of Jesus Christ (Acts 2:38).

In the eighteenth century, the Church received a new revelation regarding the righteousness of the believers. From this came two extremes: legalism and license. The first declares, among many things, that all entertainment and fashion is sin for the Christian. The opposite extreme says that the grace of God gives freedom for all things, that "for the

1 Dr. C. Peter Wagner, "Prayer and the Order of the Church," (*Global Prayer News*, April-June 2000), p. 1.

pure, all things are pure." This gives rise to the doctrine of sanctification, which for some is eternal and for others is a daily process. Perfectionism itself becomes a doctrine, meaning to some that believers cannot sin, and to others that all sin daily.

The controversy of healing as part of the propitiation of Calvary arose in the nineteenth century. The debate was whether the wounds of Christ were to provide physical healing or solely spiritual healing. Some went to the extreme belief that the only way to receive physical well-being was by faith, and so refused any medical care. Meanwhile, others were affirming that God had created medicine as the only means of healing for believers.

During that century, the eschatological doctrines of the Catholic Church spread, which included the escapist belief of the rapture and a futuristic eschatology rather than a historical one. These teachings were promoted by the Roman Catholic Church to counter the teachings of the Reformers, and still today are deeply rooted in churches that accept the teachings of Scofield, among others.

At the beginning of the twentieth century, the Church began to experience a Pentecostal awakening in Azusa, California. The doctrinal controversy over the "gift of tongues" brought a new series of doctrinal extremes. For some, if a person did not speak in tongues, that person had not received the gift of the Holy Spirit. The most extreme came to believe that if a person did not speak in tongues that person was not saved. Others believed that tongues were from Satan, not from God. During this time, the Unitarian movement also arose, also known as "only Jesus." This group believed that the teaching of the Trinity is not biblical. Others deny the unity of the Trinity and promote a concept of three gods, called tritheism.

During the twentieth century various doctrinal truths were restored to the Church. These truths were controversial for those who had taken part in the most recent movement of God. Among these were prophetic presbytery for ordination to the ministry, personal prophesy, the restoration of praise, dance, the arts, drama, and different expressions such as laughter, wailing, and being slain in the Spirit, among others.

The principles of deliverance and controversy over demon possession of believers also were re-established in this time. Some believed that a Christian could not be "possessed, oppressed, obsessed, or influenced." Others, on the other hand, attributed all situations to demons and so negated the necessity of genuine repentance of sin and the responsibility of sin due to the desires of the flesh that battle against the spirit (I Peter 2:11).

In the seventies, the Church experienced the restoration of the doctrine of blessing, inheritance, and prosperity of the saints through faith. The erroneous concept of humility as a synonym of poverty—promoted for centuries by the Church through *monasti-*

cism and *asceticism*—was replaced by the doctrine of prosperity and faith. Certainly, these truths have been a great blessing to the Church. The Holy Spirit has revealed to his people how to take hold of the necessary resources to proclaim the Gospel to all nations. However, some extremists lost the balance of the message and carried the restoration of a great truth to personal profit, leaving behind the proclamation of the gospel. Today, in spite of the fact that most of these concepts have come to a balance, some extremes continue within certain sectors of the Church.

In the 1980s and 1990s, the restoration of the personal prophetic word to the Church, to cities, and to nations has brought a renewed understanding of the ministry of prophecy and of its role in spiritual warfare for the end times. This restoration brought about, in the 1990s, the greatest prayer movement in the history of the Church.

Entire cities and nations have been shaken with the restoration of the ministry of prayer and intercession. In my book *Communities Transformed by Prayer ("Comunidades Transformadas con Oración")*, published by Betania, we present in detail the movement of God in Latin America through prayer and spiritual warfare. The video "Transformations" *("Transformaciones")*, by the Sentinel Group, shows the complete transformation of communities through the power of prayer.

The themes of spiritual warfare, spiritual mapping, and the war against territorial spirits have caused controversy in the Church today. In the same way, the lack of knowledge about personal prophecy and how to receive and examine it, have harmed some people.

False doctrines and heresies

The false doctrines and heresies that have infiltrated the Church continue to take root, and the enemy uses these to deceive and destroy.

> *But there were also false prophets among the people, even as there will be false teachers among you, who will secretly bring in destructive heresies, even denying the Lord who bought them, and bring on themselves swift destruction.* II Peter 2:1

According to the commentary in the Spirit Filled Life Bible, the word *heresies* from the Greek *hairesies* signifies "to have diversity of beliefs to create dissension and to substitute self-willed opinions for submission to the truth" (Spirit Filled Life Bible, Thomas Nelson Publishers, Nashville, TN 1991, p. 1920).

> *For there must also be factions among you, that those who are approved may be recognized among you.* I Corinthians 11:19

In the article entitled "The Decay of the Traditional Church," the magazine *Charisma* presents the numeric and theological decline of the historical denominations. Some of the deviations from biblical teaching are approaching alarming proportions. Among these, the Episcopal Church, the United Church of Christ, and the Methodist Church have taken a stand defending homosexuality. One United Methodist bishop publicly criticized the Southern Baptist Convention for its decision to reach out to the Muslims, Hindus, and Buddhists, declaring the "presumption" was "arrogant" and "assumed" that those who were not Christians were excluded from God's plan of salvation.[1] The same article made reference to the Minneapolis Conference of 1993, in which women of different denominations celebrated pagan rituals in honor of Sophia, a feminine deity, and praised "Goddess."

Witchcraft and Wicca seminars have been sponsored by The Southern Methodist University Theological School, while the Lutheran Evangelical Church continues to ordain lesbians and declare itself to be in favor of abortion and homosexuality.

In spite of these errors, extremes, and heresies, the Church is rising up as a powerful colossus to destroy the works of Satan and establish the kingdom of God here on Earth.

---

1 "The Decay of the Traditional Church," *Charisma and Christian Life,* (March 2000), p. 62.

3

The Prophetic Ministry for Revival

And it shall come to pass in the last days, says God,
That I will pour out of My Spirit on all flesh;
Your sons and your daughters shall prophesy,
Your young men shall see visions,
Your old men shall dream dreams.   Acts 2:17

In recent years, the Body of Christ has been entering a new place. For the first time—since the church of Acts—it is beginning to exercise its government from a correct biblical perspective.

During the 1970s, the foundation was laid for the ministry of intercession. After that the prophetic role began to arise, starting a divine process of establishing a new structure of church government. In a decade of severe spiritual conflict, the resurgence of the prophetic calling is equipping and directing the church toward the fulfillment of the Great Commission.

In the last years, the Lord has been raising up a prophetic and apostolic voice to the nations. Apostles and prophets were a vital part in the history of the ministry, and will be equally important in the final revival. God is restoring the foundation that is necessary for the Church to succeed in the final completion of the Great Commission.

> *Having been built on the foundation of the apostles and prophets, Jesus Christ Himself being the chief corner-stone.* Ephesians 2:20

The gift of prophesy and the office of the prophet

Two types of prophetic people exist: some have the gift of prophecy (I Corinthians 12:10) and others, the office of prophet (Ephesians 4:11).

The gift of prophecy is the supernatural ability given by God to hear and communicate that which He wishes to say to His people. The office of prophet reveals—through inspiration from the Holy Spirit—the will of God. This prophecy can never contradict the Word of God and should give testimony to the character and will of Jesus Christ.

> *Worship God! For the testimony of Jesus is the spirit of prophecy.* Revelation 19:10

A prophet is basically a man or woman who has been called by God to proclaim that which he or she perceives, sees, or hears from Him. Some

Church fathers described it as someone who had the Divine Spirit and spoke under the influence of a prophetic spirit proceeding from God. The office of prophet implies more authority than the gift of prophecy.

> *Now there are diversities of gifts, but the same Spirit.*
> *There are differences of ministries, but the same Lord.*
> *And there are diversities of activities, but it is the same*
> *God who works in all.*   I Corinthians 12:4–6

The gift and manifestations of the Spirit flow in different ways, according to the individual. Likewise, there is diversity in the styles with which prophets exercise their calling. The personality of the individual often reflects the character of his or her prophetic calling. In my life I have received prophetic words from numerous men and women of God, recognized for their prophetic ministry: men like Dick Mills, who generally prophesies using *many* passages from the Word of God, prophets like Dr. Bill Hamon, whose words flow like springs of living water from his lips, or Victor Fredes, who through his gift of teaching edifies the body of Christ. On the other hand, God has also chosen others to speak a prophetic word to cities and nations, as is the case with Cindy Jacobs.

Following, we will study some of the terms used in the Bible to describe prophets.

- **Ro'eh.** The Spirit Filled Life Bible describes it as a visionary, a seer, one who sees visions; a prophet.[1]

  "Come and let us go to the seer;" for he who is now called a prophet was formerly called a seer.

  I Samuel 9:9

- **Nabi.** One who proclaims or tells a message he has received. A spokesman, a herald or announcer. Nabi appears more than 300 times in the Old Testament. Six times the word is in its feminine form, nebiyah, and is translated as prophetess, referring to Miriam, Deborah, Hulda, Noadíah, and Isaiah's wife.[2]

  Before I formed you in the womb I knew you;
  Before you were born I sanctified you;
  And I ordained you a prophet to the nations.

  Jeremiah 1:5

  If there is a prophet among you,
  I, the LORD, make Myself known to him in a vision,
  And I speak to him in a dream. Numbers 12:6b

- **Prophetess.** One who speaks forth a divine message. At times, the message includes a foretelling of future events. Prophets are endowed with

1 *The Spirit Filled Life Bible,* (Thomas Nelson Publishers, Nashville, TN, 1991), p. 407.
2 *Ibid.,* p. 401.

insights into the counsels of the Lord, and serve as His spokesmen.[1]

So they said to him, "In Bethlehem of Judea, for thus it it written by the prophet."   Matthew 2:5

This passage makes clear reference to the prophecy of the prophet Micah:

But you, Bethlehem Ephrathah,
Though you are little among the thousands of Judah,
Yet out of you shall come forth to Me The One to be
    ruler in Israel.   Micah 5:2

This is the type of prophecy that Simeon pronounced when Jesus was brought to the temple to be presented according to Mosaic law:

Then Simeon blessed them, and said to Mary His mother, "Behold, this Child is destined for the fall and rising of many in Israel, and for a sign which will be spoken against (yes, a sword will pierce through you own soul also), that the thoughts of many hearts may be revealed."   Luke 2:34–35

• **Nataf.** A Hebrew word which means to predict, bring down from heaven, or speak through the inspiration of God. This type of prophecy is that which is generally spoken from the pulpit, or in

1 *Ibid.,* p. 1405.

a public place. It is a prophetic message given in exhortation. It is the word used in Micah 2:6, 2:11, and Zechariah 13:3.[1]

The mouthpiece of God

To be a prophet is to be a mouthpiece of the Holy Spirit. In the Bible we constantly see prayers such as: The Spirit of God *came* or *will come* and then, generally a message is presented, given by the Holy Spirit. God reveals His thoughts and plans through prophets. These men and women have the ministerial responsibility to carry the message of God to the apostles, evangelists, pastors, and teachers; who after receiving direction must share it with their disciples to put it into action.

The prophet Amos declares:

Surely the Lord GOD does nothing,
Unless He reveals His secret to His servants the prophets.
Amos 3:7

God's people can either accept or reject the message that is brought to them through the mouth of the prophet. The Scripture promises blessing for obedience and judgment for disobedience. The verb *reveal* used in this passage comes from the Hebrew *galah*. According to the Word Wealth section of the

1 C. Pierce and R. Wagner, *Receiving the Word of the Lord*, (Wagner Publications, 1999), p. 16.

Spirit Filled Life Bible, "In this reference *galah* has to do with laying bare, exposing, revealing, uncovering and disclosing His secret plan to the prophets, who are His servants."[1]

On the other hand, Scripture promises prosperity to those who hear and put into action the words of the prophets.

Believe in the LORD you God, and you shall be established; believe His prophets, and you shall prosper.
II Chronicles 20:20

The verb *believe* used in this passage comes from the Hebrew word *aman*, which signifies "to be firm, stable, established; also, to be firmly persuaded; to solidly believe . . . its most well known derivative is *amen* which conveys the idea of something 'solid, firm, absolutely secure, verified, and established.'"[2]

In the same way that God promises well-being to the obedient, He also promises judgment upon those who disobey the word of the prophets, especially prophetic messages to cities and nations. Jesus prophecied judgment over Jerusalem, a city which so badly mistreated the prophets, among them John the Baptist, who proclaimed the coming of the Messiah.

O Jerusalem, Jerusalem, the one who kills the prophets and stones those who are sent to her! How often I wanted

1 *The Spirit Filled Life Bible*, (Thomas Nelson Publishers, Nashville, TN, 1991), p. 1291.
2 *Ibid.*, p. 633.

*to gather your children together, as a hen gathers her
brood under her wings, but you were not willing!*
Luke 13:34

The cry of the prophets is to bring together the
people of God to battle and to intercede for their
cities and nations.

*Now as He drew near, He saw the city and wept over
it, saying, If you had known, even you, especially in
this your day, the things that make for your peace! But
now they are hidden from your eyes. For the days will
come upon you when your enemies will build an em-
bankment around you, surround you and close in on
every side, and level you, and your children within you,
to the ground; and they will not leave in you one stone
upon another, because you did not know the time of
your visitation.*
Luke 19:41–44

This judgment was brought upon Jerusalem in
the year 70 AD, when the Roman armies surrounded
the city and destroyed as was declared that not one
stone was left upon another.

In the New Testament the prophets continue as
the spokesmen of God. Contrary to the doctrine of
cessationism, the ministry of prophecy remains a
fundamental aspect of the Church until Christ returns for her.

*And He Himself gave some to be apostles, some prophets,
some evangelists, and some pastors and teachers, for the
equipping of the saints for the work of the ministry, for*

the edifying of the body of Christ, till we all come to the unity of the faith and the knowledge of the Son of God, to a perfect man, to the measure of the stature of the fullness of Christ; that we should no longer be children, tossed to and fro and carried about with every wind of doctrine, by the trickery of men, in the cunning craftiness by which they lie in wait to deceive, but, speaking the truth in love, may grow up in all things into Him who is the head—Christ—from whom the whole body, joined and knit together by what every joint supplies, according to the effective working by which every part does its share, causes growth of the body for the edifying of itself in love. Ephesians 4:11–16

The Lord established these ministries so that the work of the Church would conclude in the same spirit and with the same power with which it began.

Throughout the history of the Church, the ministry of the prophet has been an intrinsic part of revival and spiritual awakening.

But the center of the action of the Holy Spirit was the Church. It was there where the Holy Spirit manifested himself through the gifts of prophecy and healing, and through the casting out of demons.

Particularly, above all the manifestations of the Spirit, that of prophecy stands out. Most mentions have to do with the "prophetic spirit"[1] and its suitable use within the church.[2]

1 Pablo Deiros, *La Acción del Espiritu Santo en la Historia*, (Editorial Caribe, Miami, FL, 1998), p. 38.
2 *Ibid.*, p. 39

In his book, *The Working of the Holy Spirit in History ("La Acción del Espiritu Santo en la Historia")*, Pablo Deiros describes how the ancient writings of the apostolic fathers constantly make reference to the prophetic ministry in the daily life of the New Testament Church.

For example, Ignatius of Antioch (40?–117) refers to the gift of prophecy and his calling as a prophet in his *Letter to the Philadelphians*, saying:

> When I was with all of you, I cried out, lifting my voice, it was the voice of God . . . I knew it did not come from human flesh, but from the Spirit, that prophesied through my lips.[1]

In the days of Ignatius, in religious contexts Christian as well as pagan, it was considered a characteristic of an inspired prophet that he would speak out in a loud voice. It was assumed that one speaking under divine control should speak in as loud a voice as possible. So, in the case of Ignatius, it should not be treated as an insignificant detail, but as clear evidence that he was prophesying under the control of the Holy Spirit.[2]

Prophetic ministries have not ceased to exist;

---

1 Ignacio de Antioquía, Carta a los Filadelfos, 7.1–2—Incompleta—Ignatius of Antioch, Letter to the Philadelphians, 7.1–2, incomplete.

2 Pablo Deiros, *The Works of the Holy Spirit in History (La Acción del Espiritu Santo en la Historia)*, (Editorial Caribe, Miami, FL, 1998), p. 50. Translated from Spanish.

rather the Church has ceased to believe in them. Consequently, they have stopped working in their midst. In these times, God is reestablishing them as they are necessary to bring the Body of Christ to unity, knowledge, maturity, and collaboration necessary for growth.

Deiros notes that one of the most studied post-apostolic documents outside the Bible is *The Didache*, also known as *The Teachings of the Twelve Apostles*.

He writes about this work in his book, saying, "It is the oldest post-apostolic written work that speaks about a charismatic ministry. It is interesting to note that this early ecclesiastical manual indicates that there were prophets speaking in the Spirit and warns against false prophets in the congregation. It dedicates quite a bit of space to the ministry of prophets in the Church and presents the criteria that allows evaluation of their authenticity. *The Didache* displays a special appreciation for the prophetic ministry in particular."[1]

Simply by taking a look around us, we can tell that today is the day in which the Church is most in need of apostles and prophets.

Love never fails. But whether there are prophecies, the will fail; whether there are tongues, they will cease; whether there is knowledge, it will vanish away. For we know in part and we prophesy in part. But when that which

1 *Ibid.*, p. 56.

is perfect has come, then that which is in part will be done away. When I was a child, I spoke as a child, I understood as a child, I thought as a child; but when I became a man, I put away childish things. For now we see in a mirror, dimly, but then face to face. Now I know in part, but then I shall know just as I also am known. And now abide faith, hope, love, these three; but the greatest of these is love.   I Corinthians 13:8–13

Prophecy will cease when the perfect has come, when the Lord returns to seek His Church. The apostle John says that when we see Him, we will be like Him. The gift of prophecy will continue until the time of eternal glory arrives. In I Corinthians, chapter 14, we are exhorted to judge the prophetic word. If what is prophetically spoken contradicts the Bible, then the message is NOT from God. When someone speaks a word that is not of God, it must be stopped and corrected in a spirit of gentleness to the speaker. We cannot forget that prophetic word is proclaimed with the purpose of edification, exhortation, and consolation (vs. 3).

There are six purposes for which God sends a prophet to prepare a church, a ministry, or a nation.

1. The Church is grounded on the basis established by apostles and prophets. They have the gift of revealing God's plans for the Church, ministry, or nation. When a pastor or leader asks, "What is our future? What is my calling?" or "What problems exist that are resisting the accomplishment of this

calling?" it is fitting that an outside person be able to present the plans that God has in mind.

2. The ministerial gifts require the equipping of the saints for the work of the ministry. Prophets teach us to hear and see God. Ephesians 2:10 says, "For we are His workmanship, created in Christ Jesus for good works, which God prepared beforehand that we should walk in them."

Our function, and that of all pastors and leaders, is not only to minister to the flock but also to identify their gifts and train them in their giftings according to the Biblical patterns.

3. Prophets are gifted by God to see what goes on in the spiritual realm. Through their spiritual discernment they can recognize the powers and authorities that have been enthroned in their territories and are battling against the Church.

In I Kings 22, the people were shouting out victories and triumphs, yet Micah corrected them, declaring that a spirit of false prophecy had been sent to deceive them (vs. 28).

In II Kings 6, Jehovah permits Elisha and his servant to see the armies that are with them. Elisha shows that the armies of God are greater than those of the enemy. The prophet reveals what is occuring in the supernatural realm.

Through prophetic perception (vs. 12), Elijah informs the people of God of the enemy's tactics. The lesson here: prayer is the key to discern the strategies of our adversary. Elijah prayed and God opened the servant's eyes, and he saw (vs.17). Seeing what is unseen is the key for victorious prayer, or to discern spiritual matters from a perspective that is more divine than human, to catch a glimpse of the adversary's attack and to perceive the might of angelic attack.[1]

4. Prophets recognize and set apart leaders for the work of the ministry.

Now in the church that was at Antioch there were certain prophets and teachers . . . as they ministered to the Lord and fasted, the Holy Spirit said, "Now separate to Me Barnabas and Saul for the work to which I have called them." Acts 13:1–2

The prophet crowns the ministries of God. In I Samuel 12, we see that God sent a prophet to anoint the new king.

In my travels through Latin America and the United States the Lord gives me prophetic words for many people. I have ministered in churches where the Holy Spirit gives me words for dozens of people in the same congregation. Frequently, pastors set aside time for this administration with the leadership of the church. I can say that the Lord has given me words for thousands of people. The reward comes when, after some time, I return to a

1 *Ibid.*, p. 462.

place or I run into one of these people and they thank me for the prophetic words spoken over them and tell me how their lives or their ministries have benefited by them.

I consider my calling to be that of prophet to cities and nations. In this capacity, God sends me to many places to carry the prophetic message that I have received from Him. However, when the Holy Spirit so indicates, I administer a prophetic word to individuals He reveals to me.

5. God uses prophets to reveal his plans.

And in these days prophets came from Jerusalem to Antioch. Then one of them, named Agabus, stood up and showed by the Spirit that there was going to be a great famine throughout all the world, which also happened in the days of Claudius Caesar. Acts 11:27–28

Agabus warned the people of Antioch in advance about a great drought because he wanted them to prepare beforehand in order to help others. His word, then, was one of blessing, not of curse. He was the trumpet of alarm to an imminent danger because God wanted to prepare His people. It encourages me to see how the same passage confirms the fulfillment of the prophecy in the times of the Emperor Claudius.

Agabus is an example of the "office" of the prophet in the New Testament. This fulfillment differs from the way that the gift of prophecy works in the life of the believer, because it suggests a ministry assigned by Christ to a person, more than a manifestation given by the Holy Spirit *through* a person. We should not take lightly the office of the prophet. There is nothing in the New Testament that decreases the strict requirements which rule the fulfillment of this function.[1]

The prophet Daniel asked his friends Hananiah, Mishael, and Azariah to come together and intercede to God for him, and Nebuchadnezzar's dream was revealed to him. In his supplication to Jehovah, he blessed God, saying, *"He reveals deep and secret things"* (Daniel 2:17, 22). Later, Daniel comes before the king, saying, *"The secret which the king has demanded, the wise men, the astrologers, the magicians, and the soothsayers cannot declare to the king. But there is a God in heaven who reveals secrets . . . But as for me, this secret has not been revealed to me because I have more wisdom than anyone living, but for our sakes who make known the interpretation to the king, and that you may know the thoughts of your heart"* (Daniel 2:27–30).

The words of Daniel show that the revelation of that which is most profound and mysterious, which is hidden in darkness, is revealed by God to his prophets.

6. Through prophetic ministry the saints are edified and strengthened. Prophetic word exhorts the people of God to go forth in faith. Prophetic word,

1 Pablo Deiros, *Ibid.*, p. 1409. Translated from Spanish.

and in particular the word given by a prophetic presbytery with the laying on of hands, is equal to being set apart for the work of the ministry to which God has called us.

The prophetic ministry summons us to battle and exhorts us to break through and destroy the powers of hell.

This charge I commit to you, son Timothy, according to the prophecies previously made concerning you, that by them you may wage the good warfare. I Timothy 1:18

In II Chronicles 20:16, the prophet declares, "Tomorrow the enemy comes;" he declares how they are going to attack; and he even gives strategies to win the battle. This is how God is! He announces to us in prophecy the attacks and gives us instructions how to overcome them.

Reasons for rejection

Not everyone accepts the prophetic ministry. There are many reasons as to why the prophetic ministry has been rejected by many. On occasions, immature prophets have given words to individuals who are also immature or not yet converted, who have not known how to discern the prophetic word or simply heard what they wanted to hear and not what was spoken. Generally, a prophetic message for cities or nations is difficult to receive.

You stiffnecked and uncircumcised in heart and ears!
You always resist the Holy Spirit; as your fathers did,
so do you. Which of the prophets did your fathers not
persecute? And they killed those who foretold the com-
ing of the Just One, of whom you now have become the
betrayers and murderers. Acts 7:51–52

On the other hand, there is no doubt that the
Church has been victimized by self-proclaimed
prophets, false prophets, and independent prophets
who refuse to submit themselves to the church authorities that God has placed in a city or in a congregation. The aforementioned many times go to a city
and invite believers to private meetings, without the
covering of any church or pastoral authority. This
causes much harm to the local church and frequently
places doubt upon the calling or pastoral authority
over the Lord's flock. These "Lone Rangers" should
be avoided and confronted by pastoral leadership.
The apostle Paul writes:

Let two or three prophets speak, and let the others
judge . . . And the spirits of the prophets are subject to
the prophets. I Corinthians 14:29, 32

According to the Spirit Filled Life Bible, the
word *subject*, from the Greek *hupotasso*, signifies literally "to stand under," suggesting subordination,
obedience, submission, and subjection.[1]

1 *The Spirit Filled Life Bible*, (Thomas Nelson Publishers, Nashville, TN,
   1991), p. 1742.

The tests of a genuine prophet are his conduct and the way in which he models the ministry in his life. It is clear that one of the prophet's greatest dangers is the abuse of the ministry for personal benefit. Balaam is an example of a prophet who strays from his calling of prophecy and uses it for personal benefit.[1]

Later in the book, we will explain how the prophetic ministry always submits to the authorities that God has established in their lives: to the pastors of the congregations in which they minister and above all, to an apostolic leader under whose yoke of authority he should be. Prophets have always confronted the methods of man and have been zealous of God's ways.

They were the true intercessors who took the responsibility that the Levites had abandoned in their priestly role. For this reason, the priest always has had reservations in relation to the prophetic ministry appearing as confronting rather than collaborating. The clergy represents the control and rule of the religious mentality. The prophets were always raised by God to bring correction and conviction. I should make clear again that this is always when given under the authority established by God, to whom they submit themselves, and to whom they become accountable.

The priesthood teaches and proclaims that God

1 *The Didache*, 11.10–12.

is in the temple, whereas the prophet expresses the calling of God to leave the temple and demonstrate His power throughout the ends of the earth. The priest stays in the temple, while the prophet lives outside of it. Traditionally, the priest confronts the sheep, the prophet confronts lions, serpents, and scorpions.

The Church suffers from apathy and indifference. It has turned passive, and it is for this reason that God is restoring the prophetic ministry. The Church must wake up from its state of slumber and prepare itself for spiritual warfare. Prophets are agents of transformation. That is why the world hates them.

> *I have given them Your word; and the world has hated them because they are not of the world, just as I am not of the world.* John 17:14

Money, power, and religion are the trilogy that controls the world. The prophet makes the *status quo* uncomfortable. He confronts these powers and becomes a danger to the manipulators. For this reason also, they are persecuted and rejected.

Jesus Christ came to establish new principles and ideas, and so he had severe confrontations with the priests of His time. The prophet brings to the Church the message of what God is doing around the world, trying to awaken conviction and challenge her to establish the kingdom of God, thus fulfilling the command of the Great Commission.

THE MINISTRY AND ANOINTING OF A PROPHET

4

Prophetic Authority

John Eckhardt is an apostle and supervisor of Crusaders
Ministries in Chicago. He travels throughout the world
teaching biblical truths, "perfecting the saints" to the work
of Christ Jesus. He is author of 14 publications and produces
a daily radio and television program in Chicago, Illinois.

*See, I have this day set you over the nations and over the
kingdoms, to root out and to pull down, to destroy and
to throw down, to build and to plant.* Jeremiah 1:10

Prophets speak with a tremendous amount of authority.
The messages which come forth from their mouths
are charged with the anointing and power of God.
This authority is given to prophets by grace for two
reasons: one, awaiting the destruction of the kingdom of Satan. The other is for the establishment of
the kingdom of God.

The kingdom of darkness produces sin, rebellion, sickness and poverty; but the kingdom of God
is justice, peace and joy in the Holy Spirit (Romans
14:17). Every ministerial gift is called to take respon-

sibility in the establishment of justice, peace and joy in the Holy Spirit.

The authority of prophets gives them the ability to uproot, tear down, and destroy demonic work. Prophets also have the authority to plant and establish the kingdom of God. It is doubly emphasized in this contrast, that their authority is as much to destroy the kingdom of darkness as to build up the kingdom of God.

Those who operate under prophetic unction find themselves irreverently thrown into a spiritual war, joining in a direct conflict with the powers of darkness. The prophetic anointing often has a confrontational character.

An example of this confrontational calling is Elijah, who defied and confronted the powers of idolatry at Mount Carmel. Because of his prophetic office, he was able to overthrow the strongholds of Baal that were dominating Israel. As a result of the ministry of Elijah, eventual justice came upon the house of Ahab.

Through the message of prophets, evil spirits are rooted out from their dwellings. Remember, prophets speak with greater authority than believers who prophesy through the spirit of prophecy or with the simple gift of prophecy. The words of the prophets are like an ax laid to the root of the trees (Luke 3:9). Every tree that does not bear fruit will be cut down and thrown into the fire. Only those that have fruit and are productive for the kingdom of God will remain standing before the prophetic ministry.

Tearing Down

*For the weapons of our warfare are not carnal but
mighty in God for pulling down strongholds.*

2 Corinthians 10:4

The prophet Jeremiah had authority over kingdoms and nations. Prophets have authority over demonic realms. The prophetic unction is a spiritual
weapon the Lord uses to tear down strongholds.
Satan establishes demonic strongholds in individuals, families, churches, cities and nations.

I have seen liberation through prophecy in individuals, families and local churches. I have seen people break down and cry after receiving prophetic
messages. Prophets usually carry a strong anointing
of liberation. The prophetic ministry produces freedom and demolishes strongholds.

*By a prophet the Lord brought Israel out of Egypt, and
by a prophet he was preserved.* Hosea 12:13

The prophet has the responsibility to administer
the Word of God as well as prophesy by the Holy
Spirit. This unction instills in the prophet the ability
to call the people of God to freedom in an excep-
tional way. I have been witness to pastors who fight
against enemy strongholds in the congregation but
are unable to tear them down. The calling of pastor
is important, but demolishing certain strongholds
many times requires the support of a different

anointing, like that of the prophet. This does not elevate the prophet above a pastor in the congregation. We are all coworkers for God. Nonetheless, pastors need to discern the importance of the prophetic calling to demolish strongholds.

Uprooting

But He answered and said, "Every plant which My heavenly Father has not planted will be uprooted."
Matthew 15:13

Jesus refers here to the religious leaders of the day. His ministry offended them; a spiritual uprooting was occurring. When prophetic ministry uproots things, the people frequently will feel offended. In general, the entire religious system in Judea and Jerusalem was disturbed at its very root, provoking a dispersal of the Jewish people.

The enemy planted tare among the wheat (Matthew 13). Certain people can be planted in the Church by the enemy to cause confusion and to harm the Lord's work. The prophets have an ability to uproot them. If these roots are disturbed without the anointing, the Lord's people can end up being harmed. In this sense Jesus told his disciples not to root out the tare, lest they also uproot the wheat (Matthew 13:29).

He is uprooted from the shelter of his tent, and they parade him before the king of terrors.   Job 18:14

The uprooting of a spirit or demonic influence can not be done in the flesh. A demonic influence or spirit should be uprooted in the spirit. There are times when the prophet ignores something in the natural realm, as it is accomplishing things in the spiritual realm. It could be that the uprooting prophesied in the present won't occur until after the prophet has left the scene which could be years later. That which takes place in the natural may be the result of what has succeeded in the spiritual years ago. What we see in nature is a reflection of what is taking place or what has already taken place in the spirit.

Destroying

True prophets will destroy the works of evil. Many people, including pastors, fear the prophetic ministry. The true prophetic ministry will destroy only that which is of the enemy. It will never destroy that which is of the Lord. The things of the spirit will be established, while the things of the enemy will be destroyed.

Many of those who come to the local church are carnal, and it is lamentable to have to say that some are demonic. The prophetic ministry destroys what is of the flesh and what is demonic, and it establishes holiness and purity in the house of the Lord. Prophets hate that which is sinful because God hates it (Psalm 139:21,22).

Prophets are frequently criticized for not being

tolerant. The prophetic gift does not omit anything that must be done, because it always accomplishes its duty. A prophet who does not do so loses his effectiveness and will have to give account to the Lord. Even so, this does not give the prophet the right to be offensive, nor much less so, to minister in the flesh. Prophets should minister in the spirit at all times. A carnal prophet will end up harming what is of the Lord instead of destroying the works of the enemy.

Prophets in the flesh cause reproach and harm the same as anyone who ministers in the flesh. The true prophet has love and compassion for the people, but hates and will not tolerate the work of the enemy. The anointing will change a person into someone else (1 Samuel 10). We should not permit fighting the works of the enemy, sentencing them or being tough without a correct guide. We must discern between work in the flesh and the administration of the Holy Spirit. Without due discernment, we will wrongly judge prophets and reject them because of false understanding.

Upsetting

> *"And it shall come to pass, that as I have watched over them to pluck up, to break down, to throw down, to destroy, and to afflict, so I will watch over them to build and to plant," says the Lord.* Jeremiah 31:28

The order the nation of Israel had received was to enter the land and to tear down the pagan altars. This was part of the uprooting of the nation of Canaan because of its iniquity.

Israel had to destroy the Canaanites before they could possess the Promised Land. Prophetic anointing confronts and makes war. This is not all that prophets do; they also plant and build. But take note that before planting and building, they uproot and upset. This is a disagreeable part of the ministry; nonetheless, it is necessary.

Many prophets, in reference to this aspect, suffer internal discomfort as they feel fear and intimidation. This is disagreeable to their spirit. However, the anointing makes them into another person. The power of the calling will give you power to act above the discomfort of your spirit and will enable you to tear down those altars of sin (Hosea 8:11). In the spirit prophets—without naturally knowing anything about a congregation—can discover rebellion, control, witchcraft, and pride.

On many occasions a minister will not understand why the ministry is going in a certain direction. Sometimes the direction is totally opposite of where the ministering of the Word began. The anointing and guiding of the Holy Spirit will cause a coup in areas of sin and spiritual rebellion, many times without the minister knowing anything in the natural realm.

Building

Together with the action of destroying, uprooting, tearing down and upsetting the works of the evil one, the prophet builds up the body of Christ. This is the ministry of edification, exhortation and consolation. Prophets hate the works of evil, but at the same time have a genuine love and compassion for the people of God. The saints will be lifted up and edified through the prophetic ministry. The church will be built up, and the doors of hell will not prevail against her.

The purpose of tearing down strongholds is to build the kingdom of God. The war is not an end, but a means to accomplish the end. Prophets always should maintain their focus on the principle objective, that is to build up the church. If the prophets lose focus, they will harm the work of the Lord. The majority of prophets develop a "destructive" mentality, that is, to destroy all that is not in conformance to God.

Remember, the mission of John the Baptist was to prepare the people for an encounter with the Lord. Prophets ought not dedicate themselves solely to seeing the works of the enemy but also to seeing the needs of the people. They should balance their ministry with love and compassion. Prophets should avoid ministering with harshness, or with a critical or bitter spirit. They should have the responsibility of ministering the Word in love to the end of building the house of the Lord.

Planting

Those who are planted in the house of the Lord shall flourish in the courts of our God. Psalm 92:13

The people who live under the administration of the prophetic office will be planted in the house of the Lord. Those who are planted will flourish in all areas. To be planted means to make roots and to have a solid base. The prophetic ministry can uproot what is planted by the enemy and plant in its place what is ordained by the Lord in the Church of the Lord.

I have witnessed that many people go to church to sow doubt. The vacillations do not help in the work of the Lord. The prophetic gift ministers strength and certainty to believers to firmly establish them in the house of the Lord.

In the Church we do not need members without a foundation. We need steadfast people in the house of the Lord. Those who are firm will take root and will be like trees planted by streams of living water. The fields planted by the Lord will yield fruitful Christians. They will be constant, firm, always growing in the work of the Lord (1 Corinthians 15:58).

The more we receive the prophets, the more we will come to be trees of righteousness, the establishment of the Lord (Isaiah 61:3). I am firmly convinced that one of the reasons why we do not have many fruitful Christians in the local church is the absence of a true prophetic ministry. I have ministered for years speaking to people that they take up the calling to perfect the saints. Each ministerial gift has a divine capacity to build up the church.

Prophets have the anointing and the ability to build and to plant. Without this anointing, areas will exist where the saints are not built up and where they are not planted. Prophets have the authority of God to uproot, to tear down, to destroy, to turn upside-down, to build, and to plant. These things will come as a result of the word of the Lord which flows forth from the mouth of the prophets.

5

The Making
of a Prophet

*Now in the church that was at Antioch there were certain prophets and teachers: Barnabas, Simeon who was called Niger, Lucius of Cyrene, Manaen who had been brought up with Herod the tetrarch, and Saul. As they ministered to the Lord and fasted, the Holy Spirit said, "Now **separate to Me** Barnabas and Saul for the work to which **I have called them."** Acts 13:1–2*

Then the word of the LORD came to me, saying:
"Before I formed you in the womb I knew you;
Before you were born I sanctified you;
And I ordained you a prophet to the nations."
Then said I:
"Ah, Lord GOD!
Behold, I cannot speak, for I am a youth."
But the LORD said to me:
"Do not say, 'I am a youth,'
For you shall go to all to whom I send you,
And whatever I command you, you shall speak.
Do not be afraid of their faces,
For I am with you to deliver you," says the LORD.
Then the LORD put forth His hand and touched
my mouth, and the LORD said to me:

"Behold, I have put My words in your mouth.
See, I have this day set you over the nations and
over the kingdoms,
To root out and to pull down,
To destroy and to throw down,
To build and to plant."   Jeremiah 1:4–10

On February 2, 1976, my wife Myriam and I were invited by my brother Gabriel to visit Church On the Way in Van Nuys, California. It was in this place and on this historic date for our lives, that we had a personal encounter with the Lord. In my book *Liderazgo, Ministerio y Batalla* (Leadership, Ministry and Battles), published by Editorial Caribe, I relate the story of our calling, preparation, and separation for the ministry.

From this moment of my new birth, I had a great thirst and an incessant hunger for the Word of God. In my ministerial walk I have never taught anything unless I have complete support from the Bible. In fact, one of the first passages that penetrated my heart was the advice of the apostle Paul to his spiritual son Timothy:

> *Be diligent to present yourself approved to God, a worker*
> *who does not need to be ashamed, rightly dividing the*
> *word of truth.*   2 Timothy 2:15

Previously, Paul had told Timothy, *"Till I come, give attention to reading, to exhortation, to doctrine"*

(I Timothy 4:13), but here he says to *study* the word like a *worker* (from the Greek *ergorr* work, force).[1] Literally, to trace or divide correctly the Word of God.

For many years I prepared myself to administer the Word of God, from the moment of my conversion I felt a calling to do so throughout the whole world. I never understood God's calling on my life, as the subject of the ministry of prophet was not taught nor preached. The way in which I was using the Word seemed harsh to many. I don't think this was the ideal situation, but prophets become passionate when confronting sin and error. It was not until many years later that I could understand the nature of my actions.

On July 31, 1983, The Lord changed the course of my life. Through Dr. Bill Hamon, a prophet with a very respected ministry, God spoke to my wife and me about our calling to serve as prophet to the nations.

At that time, I found myself totally disillusioned, wounded, and frustrated. I knew that God had called me to serve Him, but it appeared that not even the church I attended recognized the calling on my life. I was passing through an emotional desert and was looking for a place where they would give me the opportunity to demonstrate the talents God had given me. Although I did not realize it at

1 *The Spirit Filled Life Bible*, (Thomas Nelson Publishers, Nashville, TN, 1991), p. 1605.

that time, God was working in me and preparing me for His purposes for my life. My character and personality frequently caused problems with others. In the church I was known as "brother sword" because many times I used the Bible to judge those who were not following its teachings or to correct doctrinal errors. Now I recognize the seal of "prophet" in this, but in many cases, I also lacked wisdom.

My theological concepts and mental predisposition were hindering me from accepting others who differed from me doctrinally. On occasion even the pastoral leadership was a victim of my attacks. It became very difficult for me to submit to a leader who in my opinion did not have the understanding or knowledge, much less the anointing of the Holy Spirit that I had.

In this search for direction for my life and my ministry, the Lord spoke to my wife and me and revealed to us His plans. What measure of love and grace to show us His purposes! He gave us the instructions we had been waiting for and showed us the steps that we should take. As if He had been reading the diary of our lives, the prophetic message examined our hearts and revealed to us that God was in control. The circumstances and situations were part of His perfect plan. All that was happening to us had the purpose of molding us into His image and likeness and of preparing us for the day in which we would be *separated* for the work of the ministry. This was the message:

You have a calling on your life to be a prophet; there is a prophetic ministry within you. It is difficult for a prophet to be under another minister. You have suffered some wounds, disillusions, and deceptions, but all of this has been part of what God has done to bring you to a dependence upon the Lord, and only on Him. Furthermore, there is an anointing of God upon you. You have passed through the experience of Moses, you have felt as though you have failed, but God is preparing you so that in HIS time you can be sent out to complete His purpose in your life. It is necessary that you submit to a relationship like that of Elisha and Elijah so that the ministry of prophecy will flow.

God has raised you up in these last days, and has put His anointing on you. You have been like Abimahaas, you have run like a guard without having all the knowledge. You have the zeal, but it is not yet your time. The hour will come in which you will be freed to pour out the glory and the power of God. Recognize that God has been in you and that you have an anointing over your life; but, do not move until you have clarity of mind and of spirit. Never move because someone says, "Move!" Consider it, but wait for a confirmation from God.

I know that there is a strong calling from God over your life. I have known many with the same calling and with the same anointing from the Lord who live jumping from one side to the other, seeking an opportunity to *shine,* and suddenly they are discouraged and frustrated, and shut down in their lament. They never succeed, because they do not submit and allow the work of God; they want to do it all by themselves, and so God works through others whom He uses to prepare them.

You have the ability to teach, inspire, and motivate people. You can lead with praise, adoration, exhortation, and motivation. You have a zeal for evangelism. Further, your calling is to be a prophet to the nations, and God is raising you up for this because He is raising up an army, not a retirement home for the elderly.

Speaking to my wife Myriam, he said:

A man's success depends greatly upon his wife. She will make or break him. Every couple can experience either heaven or hell in the ministry, based on the cooperation and help or the opposition of the spouse. The wife must make the decision of Ruth, that, "'wherever you go, I will go, and where you live, I will live.' Your ministry will be my ministry, your life, will be my life."

Speaking to the both of us, he said:

I sense in my spirit that your ministry and your lives have passed through difficult times, challenges and hard experiences; there have been adjustments, victories, and situations that have been part of the work of God. Because God has His hand over you, He will not allow you to be destroyed. They have tried to hold you back, but God is going to use them in one form or another until you can shine. The Lord is not going to give you a house with a white picket fence in the middle of nowhere without it being in the middle of His plans. I believe that you have finally surrendered to God saying, "We want to live in your perfect will!"

Later, he put his hands on us in prayer and said:

Father, as Moses laid hands on Joshua and gave him a charge, as Paul and Silas were set apart for the ministry by the laying on of hands, Lord, we set apart these two for the plans and purposes of God. We lay hands on Héctor and Myriam. You know what they have gone through; You have been with them in the midst of the challenges, the wounds, the brokenness, the pressures, the problems. We feel the fires that have surrounded them, but more, we know that You have not left them nor forsaken them.

Though they have felt alone, that nobody understands or appreciates, You have been with them always. Father, in the name of Jesus, we minister power and anointing to them from on high. We give wholeness of heart and of emotions to our sister. You have seen how her mind has suffered turmoil and confusion for things she has not understood. She has not always recognized God's dealings with her husband, and she has questioned the lack of wisdom and maturity in some of the things he has done, but she has always stayed by his side. They have had differences of opinion, but have always continued forward by the grace of God.

Lord, your anointing breaks the yokes that have tied them down. The Lord says, "I have walked with you through the valleys and the fire, when you felt alone and frustrated. I have had compassion over you and never for one moment been separated from you."

And the Lord says to you this: "My son, I have given you a spirit of discernment to identify the wolves and the true shepherds that I have put over my flock and over my ministries. I will teach you how to confide in, know, and depend on me, for there will be many to whom I call you to help, and many to whom I call you to minister. If you do not know how to confide in me, they will not confide in you and they will not depend on you. Moreover, you should forgive and free those who have failed you, who have tricked you, who have betrayed you and caused you tears and suffering. The Lord commands you to cancel the debt of those who have offended you."

And the Lord says this to you: "My son, I have put my prophetic mantel over you. I have put my anointing within and over you, and I have put over you a deposit of my glory, and I will return one day for my inheritance. I do not want you to be like the man who buried his talents and said to me, 'I was afraid, they did not give me the opportunity, doors did not open up for me.' Look not for excuses, but for obedience and submission. I want you to be like the man with the five talents who said, 'Father, I have invested, I have taken risks, I have taken steps of faith. I have set out to win others.' I tell you, son, I ask you to take steps of faith, to submit to me, turn to me, and I will pour out another measure of my anointing. I will do something new in your life; I will do a new work in your spirit. I will take you and prepare you, because I have a plan and a purpose for your life. You are my man, and you will not always understand my ways and my work, but I tell you that I am working, if I am working, and I will complete and I will perfect everything concerning you, for your times are in my hands."

After this, Dr. Bill Hamon prophesied to my wife, saying:

Myriam, the Lord says to you, "My daughter, I have called you to be comforter and consoler to this man. I have called you that you would be a balance and a help for him." At times you have thought, "Well, he is the spiritual one, he knows what to do, and it is best that I remain quiet," but the Lord says to you, "I have called you to be a mouth that speaks; you should reason with and counsel him. I have not called you to hide in your shell, nor to go to your room in silence. I have called you to speak to him and to respond to him, so that you cause him to think and to reason. Show him what the Spirit shows you and what your heart senses. My daughter, I want you to forgive with all your heart the times when he did not understand you, the times when he did not have patience with you. Sometimes the things he said to you made you feel indignant and inferior, yet the Lord says to forgive him! He has done as well as he could with his level of maturity and ability, with the weight of pressures and frustrations."

Later the Lord said to the two of us:

I want to give you a compassionate heart and a forgiving spirit, to forgive others and yourselves. Loving each other and being unified, the devil will not have space in your lives. I am restoring your matrimonial unity, your unity with me, and your unity to my calling. I love you, I have called you, and I am preparing you because your names are in my book of those whom I will be using in the last days and I have determined to put my word to work, says the Lord.

It was these powerful words, which came through the mouth of a prophet, that confirmed the calling and commission to the ministry for which the Lord had called me. It is my desire that through this book you will be able to recognize the process of calling and preparation for completing His plan in our lives, and in the same way, how the prophetic ministry is used by God to *separate* His servants for the work of the ministry.

With the passing of the years, we have understood the reasons for which God allowed us to pass through difficult times. Each one of these tests has taught us how the enemy works and how God always makes positive an experience that Satan intended to use for harm.

On February 5, 1989, at Word of Grace Church in Mesa, Arizona, the leadership of the church called together an assembly of pastors, teachers, and prophets from the city as well as an international level. The group consisted of people such as Gary Kinnaman, Dick Mills, Hal Sacks, Mark Buckley, Ron Woodworth, Leonard Griffin, Al Ells, and Robert Blayter.

The Lord gave us the following prophetic words through the mouths of these ministers.

- *From Dr. Gary Kinneman:*

You have waited for this moment for many years. I see a parallel with the life of Jesus: thirty years of preparation, service, and growth in favor before God and men. Then the anointing descends over the Lord Jesus in the waters of the Jordan. This changes His life dramatically. I see a similarity in your life. You have waited, you have been patient, even against your dreams, desires, and personal energy. You have waited and waited, and suddenly the Lord has said: now it is time. I believe that now is the time of God for your life. The multitude, the life, and the energy that has been made present in the worship of this morning are only a demonstration of what God is going to do in your ministry.

Lord, I thank you for the spirit, the anointing, the hospitality, the love, the grace, and the fervor that you have put in Hector and in his wife Myriam. Tonight you are recognizing them. It is you, Lord, who are working tonight. This is your work. I place my hands on my friend, my coworker in the gospel, and I publicly recognize him as a man gifted, mature, and a leader in the Body of Christ. We ordain Héctor and Myriam to exercise the ministry of service, teaching, prophecy, and healing. In the name of the Father, of the Son, and of the Holy Spirit.

- *From pastor Mark Buckley:*
The Lord has called the two of you to be an apostolic couple, to build on the foundations of the apostles. You will go to a church, and you will declare the Word of God to put it in order. The Lord raised you up to equip leaders and workers to establish a foundation in Christ Jesus.

- *From a pastor to pastors, Hal Sacks:*
I see that the Lord will send you all over the world, from North to South, from East to West, but the Lord promises to keep you strong and to keep you from stumbling. The strength with which He will sustain you will be your understanding of II Corinthians 2:5–6, the understanding that your power, ability, and sufficiency come from God. He has made you an able minister of His word, and He has set you apart, both of you.

• *From prophet and pastor Ron Woodworth:*

The Lord tells you this: "My people are being destroyed for lack of knowledge. Further, I am equipping you with a prophetic knowledge and wisdom. You will need the power of God where I will send you. You do know this, don't you? Like my son Jesus, who walked around doing good and healing all those oppressed of the devil. Tonight I anoint you and your wife, the companion of your youth, with a double anointing to battle against the principalities and powers and all types of spirits of darkness. Even now they are very nervous, says the Lord, because where I will be sending you, you will go in the power of the gospel of the resurrected Christ. You will not go to a place to be apologetic about the gospel. My gospel is not a myth to be discussed, but a fact to be declared, and declare it you will do. I am going to bring a celebration to your spirits that will raise the roofs in many of the places where I send you. I send you so that you may open the roofs to the outpouring of my Spirit that will consume the religiosity and will bring a sacrifice acceptable to me. I will mobilize and activate you for an aggressive evangelism, for I am sending you to save the lost and set free the captives.

• *From Dr. Al Ells:*

The Lord also remembers that recently you have had problems, offenses, and difficulties rare to your life. The cause of these has not been your flesh but the devil, who has suddenly discovered who you are. The eyes of the enemy have been opened to the anointing of God for your life. This is not so you fear, but so that you walk in wisdom and on a straight and sincere path. Allow your testimony to establish a clear victory wherever you go. The Lord gives you the victory.

- *From pastor Leonard Griffin:*

Upon hearing what the Lord says, I was compelled to remind you of the necessity of raising up a team of intercessors to pray for you. We all need prayer, but you, by nature of your ministry, are going to need a body of intercessors that will cover the two of you with prayer daily, people that intercede and stand in the gap for you. They ought to not come solely from the Hispanic ministry in your congregation, but from all the body of Christ. The Lord desires intense prayer for you two for the potential that God has for you. Call together men and women who have been faithful to you, who have loved you, and who will promise to daily stand in the gap for you, particularly during those times that you travel, which will increase in the days to come. Hear the Spirit of God say, "Pray more and pray with fervor."

- *From teacher Robert Blayter:*

God's word says that to him who is faithful in little, much will be given. No one is called to be faithful in much at the beginning. The promise is then that you will be faithful in much. You have arrived at your time to be faithful in much. In Luke 14, the parable of the great banquet speaks of a rich man who had a great dinner and invited many. However, nobody came; all who were invited had excuses. So the man sent out his servants to bring in the lame, the poor, and the blind. Having done this, they said that there was still room. I believe that you will have a great ministry here and in Latin America, but the Lord is going to build it with those whom many have deserted. You do not have to look for the great and powerful. God will use you within a ministry of restoration not only here, but around the world.

- *From a pastor to pastors, Hal Sacks:*

I see you as a young Joshua. You are not of the old generation, but of the new. The Lord says to you, "No one will rise and prevail over you. As I was with my servant Moses, so I will be with you. I will not leave you nor forsake you. Be strong and courageous. A courageous couple. I see you like a valiant lion, like the lion Aslan in the Chronicles of Narnia. Be strong, because you will cause the people to conquer the land. You will raise up my people to conquer, man of valor, but you will not go alone. Intercessors will go before you and prepare the way. And you will go and take the land."

- *From Dick Mills, prophet of the Lord:*

Enlarge the place of your tent, and let them stretch out the curtains of your habitations; do not spate;

lengthen your cords, and strengthen your stakes. For you shall expand to the right and to the left, and your descendants will inherit the nations, and make the desolate cities inhabited (Isaiah 54:2–3). *You will extend your hand to the right and to the left. And Jabez called on the God of Israel saying, "Oh, that you would bless me indeed, and enlarge my territory, that Your hand would be with me, and that You would keep me from evil, that I may not cause pain!" So God granted him what he requested* (I Chronicles 4:10). Lord, hear his request. The Lord is going to unite you in the ministry. One plants the seed, the other waters it with tears and prayer, and God gives the growth.

Do nothing without first consulting your wife. One puts a thousand to flight, two put ten thousand to flight. Say to your wife, "You represent to me the nine thousand."

Job 29:11 says, *"Though your beginning was small, yet your latter end would increase abundantly."*

Jeremiah 29:11 says, *"For I know the thoughts that I think toward you, says the LORD, thoughts of peace and not of evil, to give you a future and a hope."*

The Lord gave me a vision of a rock that falls into water and causes a ripple. As in Acts 1:8, your ministry will bring you through this city; this nation, through North America, Central America and South America, and to the ends of the earth. God will allow you to carry a miraculous ministry around the world. The Lord gave me a vision, that in the next decade,

Héctor and Myriam will be raised up and the result will be ONE MILLION Roman Catholics born again and filled with the Holy Spirit. Hallelujah!

Fruit from the ordination

Let us hold fast the confession of our hope without wavering, for He who promised is faithful.

Hebrews 10:23

More than ten years have passed since the day of my ordination into the ministry. The truth is that the prophetic words I received that day were more than my mind or my heart could take in and assimilate. Some of them even seemed to me so unbelievable that frankly, I did not see how God was going to make them a reality. Looking back and seeing what God has done in the last decade, I can say with confidence that these prophetic words have been fulfilled. As the prophet says in Habakkuk 2:3, *"For the vision is yet for an appointed time; but at the end it will speak, and it will not lie. Though it tarries, wait for it; because it will surely come, it will not tarry."*

Throughout the years, we have received many promises from God through the mouths of his prophets. Servants like Cindy Jacobs, Jim Laffoon, Mike Bickle, and many more. In the same way, the Lord has used my ministry to give word to thousands of people in various continents. Even so, I know that the ministry to which God has called me is to carry the message of God to cities and nations.

I believe that the greatest confirmation of our calling is when our friends and Christian leaders, recognized for their international ministries, publicly recognize the calling that God has given us.

In September of 1998, during a conference in Saint Louis, Missouri, a small group of prophets met to discuss the possibility of establishing a network of responsibility and relationship between some of the most recognized prophetic ministries in the nation. Taking advantage of a meeting convened by Dr. C. Peter Wagner and called the National School of Prophets, it was agreed upon to invite prophets from all "flows" of this move of God in different parts of the world to the World Prayer Center in Colorado Springs.

The meeting took place on January 27, 1999. The prophets invited to participate were a group of eighteen people, among whom were Mike Bickle and Paul Cain from Kansas City, Jim Gall from Nashville, Bill Hamon from Florida, Rick Joyner and Kingsley Fletcher from North Carolina, Jim Laffoon from California, John and Paula Stanford from Idaho, Tommy Tenney from Baltimore, Barbara Weintroble from Texas, and Cindy Jacobs, Chuck Pierce, Dutch Sheets, Mike Jacobs, Peter Wagner, and myself from Colorado Springs.

After spending an entire day in prayer and seeking the mind of Christ, He gave us a prophetic word to pray fervently, as days would come of violence in the high schools and in commercial centers. The pastors of Colorado Springs received the word with fear and mobilized their congregations and the city. Unfortunately, some pastors from the Denver area became angry and declared that the word was alarming and was not edifying, and so they ignored the prophetic message for the area. Three months later the sad tragedy of Columbine High School occurred in Littleton, a suburb of the city of Denver.

On the occasion of this meeting the Apostolic Council of Prophetic Elders (ACPE) was made official under the apostolic cover of Dr. C. Peter Wagner.

What is the purpose of the ACPE?

The prophets decided to organize ACPE in order to build positive and ongoing personal relationships among nationally recognized prophetic voices. They wanted to encourage mutual accountability and establish agreed-upon guidelines for releasing public prophetic declarations, particularly those with the potential of having widespread national or regional implications.

The ACPE is designed to establish high levels of public credibility and widely acknowledged integrity in the ministry of public prophecy. It is hoped that standards of excellence will be set not only for this generation of prophets but also for generations to come. I believe the ACPE will be used by God to create an environment in which what He desires to speak through the prophets will be heard, received, and acted upon as a normal part of the lifestyle of the Church.[1]

- *Gary Kinneman, Ph.D., author, teacher, member of the Spiritual Warfare Network. Pastor of Word of Grace Church in Mesa, Arizona.*

- *Mark Buckley, writer for Charisma Magazine, pastor of Community of Living Streams Church in Phoenix, Arizona.*

- *Hal Sacks, pastor to pastors, President of Bridgebuilders Ministry. Member of the Spiritual Warfare Network.*

- *Ron Woodworth, prophet, psalmist, pastor, and television host.*

- *Al Ells, author and director of Samaritan Counseling Center.*

- *Leonard Griffin, pastor of Covenant of Grace Church in Phoenix, Arizona.*

- *Robert Blayter, teacher.*

- *Dick Mills, international prophet.*

---

1 C. Peter Wagner, *Apostles and Prophets: The Foundation of the Church,* Chapter 8, p. 124.

6

The Fulfillment of Your Personal Prophecy

By Dr. Bill Hamon

Dr. Bill Hamon is the bishop and the founder of numerous Christian ministries. Has offices in England, Japan, Australia, Canada, and the United States. He is widely known as an apostle and prophet and the director of the largest prophetic network in the world. With more than 40 years in the ministry, he has trained more than 7,500 students and prophets in recent years. He is the author of numerous books on the ministry of the apostle and the prophet. His books on these themes are classic texts.

The majority of preachers and Christian theologians agree with the fact that there were many prophets in the Old Testament. Most also agree that prophets were the principal means of communication used by God to express his desires and purposes to human beings. Nevertheless, there are theologians who, lacking appropriate knowledge and not having experience in moving in the prophetic, have questioned the credibility of prophets and the prophetic ministry in the New Testament

Church. These, in turn, have developed strange doctrines and have suggested that when the church was established the need for having prophets and receiving prophetic ministry disappeared. Nothing is farther from the truth.

The Baptism with the Holy Spirit, the birth of the church, and the publishing of the Bible did not eliminate the need that we have to hear the prophetic voice of the Lord. On the contrary, this need intensified. Peter declared that the prophet Joel was talking about the church age when he proclaimed: " I will pour out my spirit on all flesh, and your sons and daughters will prophesy" (Acts 2:17). Paul emphasized this truth when he said to the church in Corinth: "Covet to prophesy" (1 Corinthians 14:39, Ephesians 4:11).

God still wants His will expressed verbally. For this reason He has established prophetic ministry as a voice of revelation and illumination that shows the mind of Christ to the human race. The Lord also uses this ministry to give specific instructions about how His divine will should be accomplished in a person's life. Clearly, the ministry of the prophet is not to add or omit portions of the Bible, on the contrary, it is to bring clarity and give more details about what has already been written.

This chapter is for those who have received a prophetic word, desire to understand it, and want to appropriately respond to it, so it will bear fruit. This does not mean that personal prophecy is a substitute for the responsibility and personal privilege that each Christian has to hear the voice of God for himself. It displeases God when we allow other things to take priority over the search for an intimate relationship with Him, even when this obstacle may be the ministry to which He called us. Once we have received a prophetic word from God, it is our obligation to know how to adequately respond to it.

This is the reason that I want to share six prophetic principles for responding appropriately to the voice of God. I have learned these important truths during my 39 years of experience in the ministry.

The majority of Christians do not know that just as the prophet is responsible for the declaration that he makes, the person receiving a personal prophecy is responsible for responding to it correctly. It is appropriate to point out that there are more biblical examples of prophecies that were not fulfilled because they were not responded to properly than prophecies that failed because they were simply false.

While you are studying these principles, keep in mind that the biblical basis for personal prophecy is that it is *always conditional,* even though clear terms are used in that prophetic word or certain requirements are specified.

Six Principles for Responding Appropriately to the Prophetic Word

1. A PROPER ATTITUDE. Our posture in relation to prophecy should be that of a biblical attitude, and the biblical attitude toward prophecy is totally positive. Not only does it tell us not to despise prophecies (to give them little importance), but it also exhorts us to evaluate them and hold fast to that which is good and acceptable in them (1 Thessalonians 5: 20, 21). It is even more important to know that God commands us to covet and desire the prophetic ministry (1 Corinthians 12:31, 14:39). In fact, this is the only ministry that the Bible tells us to desire.

Personal prophecy inspired by God is a specific word for an individual. The same biblical principles about the attitude that we are to have toward the written word, the *logos*, should be applied to the *rhema* that is declared prophetically. Certain conditions are essential for receiving a personal prophecy. These are:

FAITH. Basically, in order to receive prophetic ministry which comes from God with faith, our attitude toward prophets and personal prophecy should be based on the belief that this is biblical. Hebrews 11:6 says that without faith it is impossible to please God. If we receive or want to receive personal prophecy from a prophet or a prophetic presbytery we should thoroughly evaluate those who would be ministering to us. If we conclude that they have the necessary qualifications (this means that they are men and women of God who are competent in their ministry), the prophecies should be received with total confidence and belief that they are true. Believing is imperative for the fulfillment of prophecy. Hebrews tells us about the Israelites in the desert. Hebrews 4:2 says: " For unto us was the gospel preached, as well as to them: but the word preached did not profit them, not being mixed with faith" (Exodus 6; Hebrews 3:17–19). Unlike the nation of Israel, we see how Jehoshaphat believed and responded appropriately to the prophetic word declared by Jahaziel. His faith-filled response in personal prophecy resulted in a proclamation for the people of God: "Believe in the Lord your God, so shall ye be established; believe His prophets so shall ye prosper." The faith Jehoshaphat had in the prophetic word resulted in a great victory (2 Chronicles 20:22). If the prophetic declaration is received with faith, the *rhema* word that is heard will bring with it whatever is necessary for the fulfillment of that declaration: "So then faith cometh by hearing and hearing by the word of God" (Romans 10:17).

OBEDIENCE. True faith is always accompanied by obedience. James 1:22 tells us "But be ye doers of the word and not hearers only, deceiving yourselves." If in our hearing we do not progress to the point of putting into practice what we have heard, we will be easily deceived. When the Lord decides to direct us with a prophetic word, He does not do it to entertain our intellect but to give us the understanding necessary to do His will (Deuteronomy 29:29; Romans 2:13). Therefore it is much better not to receive a prophetic word than to receive it and do nothing that it commands us to do. "Therefore to him that knoweth to do good, and doeth it not, to him it is sin" (James 4:17). If we obey and do exactly what the prophetic word says, we will not be deceived and our spirit and mind will be ready to know the will of God. Jesus Christ said: "If any man will do his will, he shall know of the doctrine, whether it be of God, or whether I speak of myself" (John 7:17). If we believe and do what we should, the Lord will speak to us and will reveal more about His will for our lives.

We see a biblical example of this attitude in Noah when he received the prophetic word and obeyed it. His obedience saved his whole family (Genesis 6). On the other hand, we can see king Saul, who disobeyed the prophetic word that Samuel had given him and as a consequence his descendants lost the right to the throne of Israel (1 Samuel 15:24).

Therefore, the appropriate attitude or the correct response to personal prophecy requires obedience and cooperation. This way it will take place in our life and it will bring us to the fulfillment of God's will (Colossians 3:16).

PATIENCE. In Hebrews 6:12 it tells us that not only does faith cause us to inherit the promises but that we also need patience. These two qualities allow us to appropriate our prophetic words until the promise is obtained.

After we have received a personal prophecy and proved that it is a genuine word, we should maintain constant faith and be full of confidence that it will be fulfilled, no matter how much time passes.

At times this is not easy at all, it requires us to patiently continue seeking the will of God. If we are convinced that the Holy Spirit originated this word, we should not allow anything or anybody to steal it.

Personal prophecies are similar to precious pearls! When Jesus said we should not cast pearls before swine, he was referring to the Pharisees. We should not then bring something that God has given to us and share it with religious leaders who do not believe that God speaks today through personal prophecy. The devil can use (and he does) ministers and friends who, with good intentions, try to steal the word that God has given us. We should not let this happen. Although the prophecy causes us confusion, frustration, and discouragement due to the fact we have not seen its fulfillment, we should wait on the Lord. He will fulfill His promises! And He will transform and change our circumstances.

In Psalm 37:5–11 we have a very clear exhortation about the appropriate response to personal prophecy, especially regarding those areas that speak about ministry and about what God wants to do. We could interpret this passage this way:

"Commit your way to the Lord (the way in which your prophecies can be fulfilled), trust in it (your personal prophecy) and he will bring it to pass. Don't fret because of him who prospers in his way (the person whose ministry is growing) or because of the man who does evil (the person whose ministry is prospering and is successful, but who demonstrates lack of character, doing things his way and not according to what God says). Cease from anger (anger against God for not having answered when you wanted Him to do it), forsake wrath (forget the frustrations and the obligation you feel to cause your prophecy to be fulfilled before the appointed time) . . . but those who wait on the Lord will inherit the land . . . and will delight themselves in the abundance of peace."

Other biblical passages that clarify this divine principle are found in Hebrews 10:35–36, Psalm 27:14, and Isaiah 40:31. As a biblical example of this attitude, we see that Joseph had a vision when he was seventeen years old, but he waited patiently for God's timing (Genesis 37–42). We also find that Sarah's and Abraham's impatience regarding the prophetic promise about having an heir resulted in an Ishmael (Genesis 15:4; 16:2).

HUMILITY, MEEKNESS, AND SUBMISSION. Responding appropriately to a prophetic word also requires that the believer receive it with humility, meekness, and submission. If we decide to accept a prophetic word but we respond to it with pride, anger, doubt, resentment, criticism, self-justification, or arrogance, we reveal a state of immaturity or a wrong spirit. We should understand that a wrong attitude tends to neutralize what God has declared that He wants to do.

Sometimes we have preconceived ideas about the great ministry that we believe God will confirm through a prophet. When God does not talk to us about our desires to be famous, then we are disillusioned, depressed, and even angry with him. Many times we insist on thinking that the prophet or the presbytery made a mistake or didn't know how to discern the mind of the Lord.

On some occasions, the words that the Lord gives through prophecies require changes in our behavior and attitudes. James 1:21 says: "Receive with meekness the word." We should be ready to respond with wisdom. The Bible tells us that if we admonish a wise man he will be wiser, but if we admonish a fool, he will hate us. A person who is mature and has a proper attitude, will respond appropriately to a personal prophecy even when it is a word of correction, demonstrating in this way the attributes of heavenly wisdom: "But the wisdom that is from above is first pure, then peaceable, gentle, and easy to be entreated, full of mercy, and good fruits, without partiality, and without hypocrisy" (James 3:17).

Finally, pride can prevent personal prophecy from being fulfilled. We find an example in 2 Kings 5 when Naaman, the general of the Syrian army who was a leper, wanted the prophet Elisha to heal him. When Elisha sent a messenger to Naaman telling him to go and wash in the Jordan so he would be healed, he became angry. His personal pride was wounded because Elisha had not gone out to receive him and his sense of national pride was hurt because the Jordan was in Israel and not in Syria. The biblical passage tells us that in the long run Naaman humbled himself and obeyed Elisha's instructions and his obedience to the prophetic word produced healing. Naaman's disposition to lay his pride aside and act in obedience activated the prophecy so it would be fulfilled.

2. RECORD, READ, AND MEDITATE ON YOUR PROPHECY. One of the important principles for responding appropriately to personal prophecy is taping what has been said and then transcribing it in order to be able to read it and meditate on it. The apostle Paul told Timothy: "Neglect not the gift that is in thee, which was given thee by prophecy, with the laying on of the hands of the presbytery. Meditate on these things; give thyself wholly to them; that thy profiting may appear to all" (1Timothy 4:14–15). In this biblical portion, Paul was reminding Timothy that he had received a gift through prophecy, when the prophetic presbytery had ministered to him. In addition he reminded him not to neglect the gift that was in him. Paul also told him to meditate on his personal prophecies so all that had been declared might come to pass and be a benefit to the whole Body of Christ.

This causes us to ask: How would Timothy be able to meditate on the words that had been declared over him by the prophetic presbytery, unless he had written them? It appears, those close to Timothy knew the biblical precedent of writing down and meditating on what God had said. The following Bible passages show us how important it is to write down and meditate on the prophetic word: Habakkuk 2:2; Revelation 2:1; Isaiah 8:1; Jeremiah 36:2; Ezekiel 2:10; 3:1–3; Zechariah 5:1–4; Joshua 1:8; Psalms 1:2; 19:14; 39:3; 63:6. Many of the prophecies that I received in the first years of my ministry (in the 50s and 60s) could not be recorded on tape due to the inaccessibility of sound equipment. Even so some of the prophecies were taped on 7-inch cartridges that were then transferred to smaller ones and were finally written. Nowadays we can tape more easily and we always should make use of these resources when we are ministering a personal prophecy.

When we do not give sufficient importance to taping the prophetic word, it loses its value with time since the details of the prophecy are easily forgotten. This becomes more evident when the prophecy is extensive. Personally, I only remember two or three sentences of the thousands of words that were prophetically declared over me and that were never taped. In summary, we cannot respond to personal prophecy adequately unless we have taped, read, and understood it clearly.

For this reason adequate preparation is required before ministering. When the prophetic presbytery ministers, they will normally make the necessary preparations for taping everything.

Another of the benefits that we can receive from having the prophecy taped is that we can compare it with other words that we have received previously. In general, prophetic words tend to share the same idea, or make use of similar words without it mattering that the prophetic words come from different people who have no prior knowledge of what has been said on other occasions. This prophetic harmony confirms that the words are genuine and that they come from the Lord, because they are being confirmed by the mouth of several witnesses.

Besides benefiting the person who receives the prophetic word, taping protects the prophet. Some people misinterpret or twist what they hear or what they believe they heard in prophecy. What they remember then can be applied according to the egotistical desire of the person and not according to the will of God.

Another advantage of taping, writing, and meditating on personal prophecy is that it reveals to us the possibility of the word having more than one interpretation. Many times the way we initially understand the word is not the most appropriate or true interpretation. On one occasion I visited a minister in order for him to give me a prophetic word concerning a financial need that I had and that was very urgent. At that time I was behind on the payment of a $40,000 debt. The prophecy that I received said, "I will supply your need, because to deny you would be to deny myself." I left there confessing that the Lord had supplied my need but that was not the case. Later I asked the Lord why he had not fulfilled his promise. The Lord answered, "Yes I did. I gave you the provision I promised you through my servant. You believed that your greatest need was that payment, but I saw a greater need than money and I faithfully fulfilled it. Then the Lord illuminated my mind so I could understand the greater provision that God had given me that night. In light of this example, we should always review the prophecies, whether it is with the pastor or an elder of the church that believes in and understands personal prophecy. Other people can also help us to be sure that we are not changing the message or misinterpreting the prophecy.

Finally, knowing that we should tape, write, and meditate on the prophetic word, we have to understand that we should not make important decisions or arrive at quick conclusions that are based upon the prophetic word that we are receiving at that moment. When we receive a prophetic word, it is better to listen attentively, in an attitude of prayer, and without arriving at conclusions before having the opportunity to transcribe it. At the time of receiving the ministry, we should remain attentive to the Spirit when He is giving witness about the spirit of the prophet and of His divine inspiration and motivation instead of judging or evaluating the prophecy at that moment. Some conditions, such as our emotional and mental state and our physical posture can be barriers that prevent evaluating the prophecy correctly.

3. BEARING WITNESS TO THE PROPHECY.
How can we know that the prophetic word is true?

In the same way that we know that we are sons of God: "The Spirit himself bears witness with our spirit. (Romans 8:16). Prophecies are tested according to biblical principles and by using adequate criteria to judge them. Nevertheless, we primarily bear witness to the prophecy in our *spirit*.

Sometimes I have heard people say: "I didn't feel the witness of the Spirit about that word." But after questioning them, I understood that some of them wanted to convey that the prophecy did not accommodate their theology. Others did not like what had been said and they reacted negatively to what had been prophesied. In these cases, they made the mistake of assuming that we bear witness with our carnal mind or with our emotions or with our will or according to our own opinion, desires, or objectives.

In order to be able to bear witness to a prophetic word, we should discern between soul and spirit. Man's spiritual sphere is the place where divine love and faith operate; the soul contains our emotions, will, imagination, and desires, and the flesh conforms to the five senses and includes our feelings.

Our reasoning is in the mind, not in the spirit. Due to this, our traditions, beliefs, and opinions should not be used as a basis for accepting prophetic truth. In reality, these faculties frequently bring doubt, confusion, resentment, rejection, and rebellion against true personal prophecy. Sometimes our mind says "no" while our heart says, "follow". The soul tells us "I don't understand!" while our spirit says: "Trust in the Lord with all thine heart and lean not unto thine own understanding. In all thy ways acknowledge him and he shall direct thy paths" (Proverbs 3:5–6).

As an example, let's consider what would happen if a devout Catholic received a prophecy saying not to worship Mary. Would he be in agreement with that word? Probably not, and he would reject it due to his tradition and his devotion to the Virgin Mary. Likewise, if you prophesied baptism by immersion in water to a Presbyterian, or speaking in tongues to a traditional Baptist all would react in the same way.

The problem confronting us today is that many Christians do not know how to discern between the negative reactions of the soul and the absence of the witness of the Spirit. The reaction of the Spirit originates in the depths of our being. Some believers say that the physical manifestation is a sensation in the "gut" or in the lower part of the chest. When the spirit reacts to something negative, it is usually manifested by nervousness, uneasiness, or with an inexpressible feeling that tells us that something is not right. This is the spirit telling us, " No!", "Be careful!" or "Something is not right!"

We can "read" these reactions correctly when we are more in tune with our spirits than with our thoughts. If it is the mind that provokes them, then it is possible that we are having a soulish reaction instead of the witness of the Spirit.

When the Spirit of God witnesses positively to our spirit that the prophetic word is correct, that it comes from God, and that it agrees with His divine purpose and will, then our spirit will reflect the fruit of the Spirit. There will be deep peace, an unexplainable joy, and a sensation of love and rejoicing. This sensation is the confirmation that the Holy Spirit is bearing witness to our spirit that all is in order, even though we may not understand everything that is said to us or our soul cannot immediately grasp everything that has been declared.

Do not take action if you do not have the witness of the Spirit. If there is no reaction or sensation in your spirit, and you only have a neutral feeling inside, then you should "wait and see." If the Spirit says no: " There is no reason to get upset or to worry." We should wait and in the meantime we should trust, obey, believe, and do what we know we should do. If the prophecy is from God, it will be fulfilled and in this way we will carry out the will of God.

Finally, in order to test the prophetic word, it is necessary to understand the concepts *new revelation and confirmation*. Unfortunately, some teach that prophecy is only to confirm. This teaching suggests that we should reject all those personal prophecies that present a totally new idea. This line of thinking adds that God only speaks prophetically about things that we have already felt in our spirit and that this is the confirmation. This would be the ideal, but it isn't always what happens.

Without doubt some prophecy is easier to receive and bear witness to when it is a confirmation of what has been received before. Nevertheless, I believe that we deceive ourselves when we insist that God must speak to us first and when we think that He will never inspire a prophet to declare something totally new to us. In reality, I believe that when we think this way, we are exalting our own ego. We are saying that God always has to submit to this method before He is able to speak to us through another person. This belief has no biblical basis.

We can present some biblical examples that demonstrate that God can declare something new to a person through a prophet. For example, David, the young shepherd, was anointed by Samuel who prophesied that he would become king. Nowhere do we find evidence that this young man had dreamed of being the king of Israel.

We cannot reject the word of the prophet or consider it incorrect simply because we have not considered the possibility of what is being prophesied. God uses the prophets to express new truths not only to the church but also to people. We should examine all prophetic words in depth before we reject them.

When we receive a new revelation through a personal prophecy, it is best to consider the word, write it, and pray over it. We should also wait and see what happens; we should be flexible, accessible, and have an open heart. When God opens the doors in the indicated area, we then know that it is of God because we have received the confirmation from

Him. Many times the prophetic confirmation arrives before we realize that we need it.

4. FIGHT THE GOOD FIGHT. "This charge I commit to you, son Timothy, according to the prophecies previously made concerning you, that by them you may wage the good warfare" (1 Timothy 1:18). Paul told Timothy that he should do more than just meditate on the prophecies: he told him to use them for war. We can take the personal prophecies that we have seen and proven to be true and we can wage war by standing on them. The kings of Judah and Israel, like David and Jehoshaphat, conquered their enemies when they trusted in the personal prophecy that they received from the prophet.

Joshua also received a specific word about the city of Jericho and we see how these words declared to him and to Jehoshaphat provided the strategy for them to do what they had to do in God's exact timing. This kind of word can be considered a personal prophecy. They obtained the victory because the leaders followed the specific direction that the Lord had given them for that situation in particular.

Warring spiritually implies constancy and personal prophecy gives us the power to persevere. The Apostle Paul withstood great sufferings with joy because a servant of God had prophesied to him that he would suffer those hardships for the cause of Jesus Christ. "For I will show him how many things he must suffer for my name's sake" (Acts 9:16).

If we can take the prophecy that we have been given and war with it spiritually, we know it brings God's perfect will as a result. If we trust in God, we will be blessed, but we should also believe what the prophets say in order to prosper (2 Chronicles 20:20).

5. DO NOT MAKE A DEFINITE DECISION UNLESS YOU RECEIVE SPECIFIC INSTRUCTIONS.

When a person receives a prophecy that makes reference to what God is going to do in his life or the call that he or she has, what should he do?

Let's look at an example. A young man who has consecrated himself to the Lord and is studying law, receives a personal prophecy that says that he has been called to be a pastor. Should he stop studying and go into the ministry? Should he finish his studies? Should he change his career? In short, upon considering all his options, what would be the correct way to respond to the word given?

According to the biblical pattern, this young man should not change anything unless specific instructions are given. If God does not give us concrete direction about what we should do, it is better to keep on doing what we were doing before we received the prophetic word. We should keep this in mind even though someone has told us that we will do exploits in the future. David was called from where he was shepherding the sheep, and Samuel anointed him as king over Israel. But the Lord did not tell him how or when this would be fulfilled.

Neither did He tell him the steps that he would have to follow. It was simply a prophetic declaration. After this ceremony, David returned to the ministry of shepherding the sheep, practicing with the sling-shot, and learning to sing and play the harp in order to minister to the Lord. David received the word that he was going to be king at an early age and during that time the only thing he could do was wait on the timing of God and keep himself occupied until the day on which the prophecy would be fulfilled (1 Samuel 16). All true prophecy that speaks about future time, even our prophecies, should wait on God's timing for its fulfillment.

On the other hand, when the prophecy received includes specific instructions and an anointing for taking immediate action, we should then do what we are told to do (2 Kings 9). For example Jehu, one of the captains of the army of Israel, received this type of prophecy. Elijah commissioned one of his prophets to take a cruse of oil to Ramoth Gilead and there he should anoint Jehu as king of Israel, and then he had to flee. This messenger not only anointed Jehu but he also prophesied the destruction of the dynasty of Ahab, which Elijah had prophesied before.

6. KNOW GOD'S UNIVERSAL PRINCIPLES. God has divine requisites, directives, and principles that must operate in proper order so that the things He establishes may work. Just as there are natural laws in the universe and in nature, there are also biblical and spiritual laws that show us how to obtain and supply our personal and ministerial needs.

In order to form water you have to have the correct combination of hydrogen and oxygen (H_2O). For a plane to fly, it must have the correct design and thrust. These must conform to the laws of aerodynamics in order to surpass the law of gravity and to be able to take off, maintain a controlled flight and land normally. Personal prophecy is like the plane, our capacity to accomplish what has been declared depends on the fulfillment of certain laws.

For example, imagine that someone gives you an automobile to take a trip around the country. Do you think that just having the car guarantees that you will arrive at your destination? No! You as the driver have the responsibility of taking the necessary precautions so that the automobile will take you where you want to go. You must keep the fuel tank full, the motor oiled, the water in the radiator, and the tires in good condition. The fact that you have received a personal prophecy that has shown you what to do, or who you will become, or how you will accomplish your personal and ministerial goals does not guarantee that you will arrive at the personal realization of that declaration.

In order for that to happen, you must keep your "car" full of the fuel of faith and obedience. You must take precautions to have the right amount of the oil of trust and keep the appropriate level of the water of joy.

Personal prophecy is similar to the process of preparing a cake. All the necessary ingredients have to be added in adequate proportions, they must be mixed together until they have the appropriate consistency, and afterwards the cake must be cooked in the oven for the adequate amount of time. Only after this process will the cake have the shape and flavor that will cause others to want to enjoy it.

Personal prophecy is like getting answers to our prayers. Jesus declared, "Ask and it shall be given unto you." "Most assuredly, I say to you, whatever you ask the Father in my name He will give you" (John 16:23). Even so many Christians "ask" in prayer but they never receive answers. Are Jesus' words false or wrong when Christians declare this verse and nothing happens? Should we lay this verse aside and say it is not from God because we don't receive an answer? Of course not! For prayer to be answered, just as when you are making a cake, you must have the necessary ingredients and not just an act of "asking" alone.

James declares: "You ask and do not receive, because you ask amiss, that you may spend it on your pleasures" (James 4:3). Here we can see what the additional ingredients are: asking correctly and with the proper motive. Other biblical passages such as Mark 11:24 and Hebrews 11:6 reveal that faith must be added to our prayers in order for them to be answered.

In the same way, this can be applied to personal

prophecy. There are certain attitudes and actions that must be mixed together and left in "the oven of God's timing" before they can be fulfilled. Just as the car needs maintenance to be used as a means of transportation, personal prophecy will not be fulfilled unless we learn to respond correctly to the voice of God.

In summary, I want you to memorize and meditate upon the appropriate responses to personal prophecy until you incorporate them into your life and ministry. Trust in the Lord so you will be established, believe in personal prophecies and fight the good fight with them so you can prosper and be victorious in your life and in your ministry.

From these prophetic guidelines we can conclude that it is not sufficient to just receive a prophecy. We must also respond correctly in order to see its fulfillment. Let's review these six principles. We must:

1. Have the correct concepts about faith, obedience, patience, humility, meekness, and submission
2. Be willing to tape, read, and meditate on the prophetic words that we have received
3. Learn to discern correctly in order to be able to bear witness to our prophecies
4. Be willing to fight the good fight
5. Not make a definite decision unless we receive specific instructions to do so
6. Know God's universal principles

7

Forerunners of Change

G od sends the prophet in response to the clamor of his people. They prepare the way for a fresh awakening of God, they prophesy life where there is none, and they prepare hearts for a special visitation from on high. When a generation appears to be without life or hope, there is always a remnant of faithful men and women who serve and pray to the Lord for an outpouring of his Spirit, for changes in a sinful and corrupt society that has turned away from Him.

In the times of Zacharias, the people of Israel were living under the hand of the Roman conquest. Jehovah had not spoken to his people in more than four hundred years. The prevailing conditions were of chaos and hopelessness. Nonetheless, we find a faithful number who intercede before the throne of God and a priest who offers incense in the sanctuary.

> *So it was, that while [Zacharias] was serving as priest before God in the order of his division, according to the custom of the priesthood, his lot fell to burn incense when he went into the temple of the Lord. And the whole multitude of the people was praying outside at the hour of incense.* Luke 1:8–10

The passage tells us that Zacharias is found praying in the temple, interceding as he offered incense and intercession (Psalm 141:2). At the same time, outside the temple we find a multitude that also was crying out to Jehovah.

We find many examples in the Bible that indicate that God responds to the cries of His people. Whenever Israel was in times of crisis and a servant cried out to Jehovah, God would send an angel to assure them that their prayers had been heard and generally, in response, He would send a prophet to prepare the people for a special visitation.

> *But the angel said to him, "Do not be afraid, Zacharias, for your prayer is heard."*   Luke 1:13

The answer was the arrival of the prophet John, a name that signifies favor and grace. John was the *forerunner* of Jesus, that is, he came beforehand to prepare the people for the coming of the Savior (Luke 1:16–17). Even so, when Jesus came, the people did not recognize Him. Then, weeping over the city of Jerusalem, Jesus proclaimed judgment over them.

> *Now as He drew near, He saw the city and wept over it, saying, "If you had known, even you, especially in this your day, the things that make for your peace! But now they are hidden from your eyes. For the days will come upon you when your enemies will build an embankment around you, surround you and close you in on every side, and level you, and your children within*

you, to the ground; and they will not leave in you one stone upon another, because you did not know the time of your visitation." Luke 19:41–44

O Jerusalem, Jerusalem, the one who kills the prophets and stones those who are sent to her! How often I wanted to gather your children together, as a hen gathers her brood under her wings, but you were not willing! Luke 13:34

The cry of the prophets is to unite the people of God. They desire that the people repent and seek the face of God so as to be able to receive His grace and favor. John the Baptist presents himself before a captive nation, but one that has a remnant of intercessors crying out in prayer for mercy from Jehovah. The fiercest opposition he encountered was from the religious order, specifically the priests and Levites. All those who were part of the "religious head" of the people saw with fear the possibility of losing control of the people of God.

Because of this, God raised up prophetic forerunners to call idolatrous and sinful people to repentance, to raise them from the valley of dry bones and to prophecy life over them.

Son of man, set your face toward the mountains of Israel, and prophesy against them. Ezekiel 6:2

So I prophesied as I was commanded; and as I prophesied, there was a noise, and suddenly a rattling; and the bones came together, bone to bone. Indeed, as I looked, the sinews and the flesh came upon them, and the skin covered them over; but there was no breath in them. Then He said to me, "Prophesy to the breath, prophesy, son of man, and say to the breath, 'Thus says the Lord GOD: "Come from the four winds, O breath, and breathe on these slain, that they may live."'" So I prophesied as He commanded me, and breath came into them, and they lived, and stood upon their feet, an exceedingly great army. Ezekiel 37:7–10

Intercessory prayer brings forth a prophetic Spirit. The Scriptures tell us that Zacharias was filled with the Holy Spirit and prophesied, saying:

Blessed is the Lord God of Israel, for He has visited and redeemed His people. Luke 1:68

Anna was another one of the forerunners to the visitation of the Messiah. Scripture tells us that she was a prophetess advanced in age, widowed for eighty-four years, and servant of God with a spirit of intercession who served in the temple with fasting and prayers (Luke 2:36–38). Today, just as with John the Baptist and Anna, God is raising up the prophetic ministry and ministers in the role of prophets as forerunners for the greatest visitation in the history of the Church. We are entering into a new time, a new generation, one that we believe will possibly be the last. If this is true, the Church is living in moments of preparation for the return of the Lord. The Church has the prophetic calling of announcing the coming of the Lord, of calling to repentance, and of declaring publicly to the authorities their sin, just as John the Baptist did with Herod.

God's promises for the end times include an unprecedented outflow of the Spirit of God over the whole face of the earth. The promise is that the entire earth will be full of the knowledge of the glory of God. The promise of a latter rain greater than the first brings us to the days in which we live. What the disciples saw and did in the book of Acts is only a guide so that the Church of the end times—which is the present church—may have a pattern to establish the Kingdom of God on earth.

The prophetic ministry and the role of the prophet are part of the necessary foundation to awaken the Church to her calling of spiritual warfare and intercession. This is the way of putting the enemy under our feet (Hebrews 10:13, I Corinthians 15:23–25), destroying the works of evil, and establishing the lordship of Christ on the earth. Once this is accomplished, Christ will come to reign over all the earth and thus will remain forever and ever! (Revelation 11:15).

The *forerunner* is He who is sent to stand in the gap, to open the field, to level the ground. Nonetheless, each time the prophetic message of God is brought to regions, cities, and nations, strong opposition arises from the religious institutions and ecclesiastical leadership. Many times this is owed to the fact that the pride and desire for power prevent them from seeing that which is occurring. Their heart is hardened to receiving a fresh move of the Holy Spirit. All of this resistance is based in the lack of knowledge that the Church has had about the role of prophecy. In these times we are witnesses of the restoration of this ministry so important for the fulfillment of the Great Commission.

The recognition of the prophetic ministry has stretched leaders in the Body of Christ from their comfort zones. Its message of sounding the trumpet and giving the alarm is not accepted by those who have based their ministries, empires, and mega-churches on the promises of God which are conditional upon faith and obedience. Some are quick to forget the judgment of God upon cities and nations and ignore the messages of the prophets who speak in behalf of the God of peace and justice. He is the Lord who promises to pour out his judgment over the nations of this world.

Forerunner in Latin America

For more than a decade the Lord has sent us to numerous cities and nations to declare the prophetic message of God for them. The story of our ministry has been time and again that of being in the forefront and calling together the people of God to unity, intercession, and spiritual warfare.

In this pilgrimage the Lord has carried us to Asia, Africa, Europe, and all of America, and I can say that in the majority of the occasions that I can remember, we were invited to carry out the *first* congress, the *first* seminary, the *first* conference, the *first* workshop, etc., in the themes of intercession, spiritual warfare, prophecy, the apostolic movement, among others. As in all new projects, initially we have received little support, and in some cases severe opposition from the established leadership. This is to be expected. Such was always the case in the Bible.

In cities such as Cali, Panama, Maracaibo, La Paz, Santo Domingo, and others, the leadership has embraced with joy the message of God. As a result, processes of transformation have begun in these communities that are well-known throughout the world. This reminds me of the story of Ninevah and its receptiveness to the message of the prophet Jonah that brought about the forgiveness of God over judgment already decreed due to the repentance, intercession, and fasting of the inhabitants of the city.

On the other hand, in cities like Medellin, Mexico, Caracas, Asuncion, Lima, Miami, among others, the receptivity has not been the same. In these places, with the exception of Medellin, they are still far from experiencing a visitation from God, though this now is beginning to change. It is good to remember that the fall of Jerusalem into the hands of her enemies was due to her open opposition to the prophets.

In North American cities like Toronto, New York, Boston, and Reno, God has used us through the Hispanic church to begin a process of transformation and to establish a vision of the lordship of God in them.

Communities and entire nations are experiencing a visitation from God, and as a result, have begun their process of transformation. This produces in the individual or in the community a realignment of forces, as much political as religious. It directs our efforts to achieve a goal and on the other hand, we see confrontation occur with the opposing forces. When this happens, the Church is called to be forceful and not to be intimidated by its adversaries. When the Church, in the confidence of its mediator and advocate, resists the attacks, it soon experiences freedom coming from the hand of God.

The Church in Colombia is a perfect example of this. Today this beautiful country is living through difficult times as a result of great opposing forces sustained by the powers of darkness to resist the visitation from God. The word of life and hope is that history shows that adversity and persecution produce incredible growth.

The times in which we live challenge the Church not only to keep what it has, but also to take possession of that which it does not have. The moment has come to reclaim the land that God has given us! And for this, it is necessary to listen to the prophets.

Believe in the LORD your God, and you shall be established; believe His prophets, and you shall prosper.
                                                    II Chronicles 20:20b

The non-Christian world is crying out for a prophetic voice for the times in which we live, and as they are not finding it in the churches, they run to those who practice the occult, parapsychology, and divination. We have to realign our lives and our ministries to the flow of the river of God. The order of God for His Church is to enter into battle with a promise of victory and not of defeat. Now is not the time for negotiation for a peace agreement. The God of peace has already won the war on the cross and promises to crush His enemies.

8

The Apostle in the End Times

My studies of church-growth have led me to an inexorable conclusion: The fastest-growing identifiable segment of Christianity in the 1990s on five continents is what has come to be called the Postdenominational Movement. Inherent in today's postdenominational churches is a structure commonly known as "apostolic networks," in which both the gift and the office of apostle are recognized and accepted.

Dr. C. Peter Wagner[1]

For many years the ministry of the apostles has been ignored by the Church. Today we see how God is raising up throughout the world a new generation of leaders who are recognized for their gifts and callings as apostles in the Church. These have a commission and a commitment with their calling and can say with the apostle Paul, "I was not disobedient to the heavenly vision" (Acts 26:19).

I definitely believe that David Cannistraci says

---

1 Cannistracci, *Apostles and the Emerging Apostolic Movement*, (Renew Books, 1996), p. 12.

it better than anyone: "I do not believe that the apostles are more important than any of the other ministries like pastors or teachers, but I do believe that they are as important. Further, without the restoration of apostles the other ministries are incomplete. Now is the time for us to bring apostles into focus in the Body of Christ and to include them with the other essential gifts Christ has given us."[1]

In order to comprehend the significance of the apostolic ministry it is necessary that we first understand the significance of the word apostle. In the past, many have considered the word to mean the same as *missionary*. This latter word is derived from the Latin *missionarius* and is defined as one sent to do a religious work in another culture, and its significance is different than in the Greek text.

Dr. Wagner defines the labor of a missionary as "the special capacity that God gives to certain members of the body of Christ to administer whatever other spiritual gift that they may have to a second culture."[2] In the same way, he insists on the difference between the ministries of the apostles Peter and Paul. Peter, as an apostle to the Jews, did not cross cultures, while Paul was called to go to the Gentiles, for this reason he was not only an apostle, but also a missionary.

The Greek term which translates to apostle is

1 *Ibid.*, p. 19.
2 C. Peter Wagner, *Terremoto en la Iglesia*, (Caribe/Betania Editores, Miami, FL, 2000), p. 109.

apostolos, and its root is translated as someone who is *sent* from one place to another to accomplish a specific work. In ancient times it was used to describe a marine officer, generally an admiral or an individual responsible for a flotilla of ships. It was also used to refer to an *emissary* or an *ambassador.* When the ships set sail to establish a new colony, the admiral and his crew were called apostles.

Apostles are the delegates for a mission. They represent their commanders and carry out their orders. The words *apostolos* and *apostellos* literally mean *messengers* or *envoys.* The term apostle appears seventy-nine times in the New Testament and of these, twenty-eight are in the book of Acts and thirty-eight are in the other epistles. On some occasions it has been interpreted as *messenger.*

If anyone inquires about Titus, he is my partner and fellow worker concerning you. Or if our brethren are inquired about, they are messengers of the churches, the glory of Christ. II Corinthians 8:23

Yet I considered it necessary to send to you Epaphroditus, my brother, fellow worker, and fellow soldier, but your messenger and the one who ministered to my need. Philippians 2:25

In the Spirit Filled Life Bible, the word *apostolos* is defined as "a special messenger, a delegate, one commissioned for a specific assignment or function, one who is sent forth with a message. In the New

Testament, the word refers to the twelve original disciples and other predominant leaders outside of the twelve."[1]

In Ephesians 4:11–16 we are told that it is one of the gifts given to perfect the saints for the work of the ministry and for the edification of the body of Christ. In the book, *Los dones espirituales y cómo pueden ayudar su iglesia (Spiritual Gifts and How They Can Help Your Church)*, Dr. C. Peter Wagner defines the term like this:

> The gift of the apostle is the special ability that God gives to certain members of the body of Christ that allows them to assume and exercise leadership over a number of churches with the extraordinary authority in spiritual matters that is spontaneously recognized and appreciated by those churches.
>
> The apostle is the person whom God has given to the pastors and leaders of the Church. He is the person to whom these all go to seek counsel and help. He is able to smooth out animosities and bring peace, to find the cause of what has gone wrong, to resolve problems. He can make demands that seem autocratic, but that are accepted willingly by the Christians, as they recognize his gift and the authority that goes with him. His vision is well focused, and he is not restricted by the problems of a local church.[2]

---

1 *The Spirit Filled Life Bible*, (Thomas Nelson Publishers, Nashville, TN, 1991), p. 1738.
2 C. Peter Wagner, *Sus Dones Espirituales Pueden Ayudar a Crecer su Iglesia*, (Libros Clie, 1980), p. 206.

The apostolic ministry is raised by God to bring reforms. He first gives the revelation of the lost or hidden and then launches reform for that which has not been functioning. The apostles are pioneers; they open the gap so that the truths of God can flow through freely.

The apostle John Eckhardt writes in his book *Moving In the Apostolic,* "Apostles have the anointing to defend and confirm the faith. They walk in resolve to proclaim the truth before and despite all opposition and persecution. This is what God is restoring to the Church. He does not allow this to confuse or surprise him."[1]

The apostles of the New Testament are the judges of the Old Testament. God's desire has always been to govern and direct His people through His judges. God gives this gift of judgment and the ability to make decisions according to His will.

The word "judge" means to give direction, to issue verdicts. Thus, Paul judges the spiritual condition of the churches in Corinth and Ephesus and gives them direction to institute the necessary reforms.

The prophet Isaiah declares:

I will restore your judges as at the first,
And your counselors as at the beginning.
Afterward you shall be called the city of righteousness,
   the faithful city.

1 J. Eckhardt, *Moving in the Apostolic,* (Eckhardt, 1999), p. 83.

Zion shall be redeemed with justice,
And her penitents with righteousness.

Isaiah 1:26, 27

When he speaks of judges in this passage, he refers to the apostles, and when he mentions counselors, then he is making reference to the prophets. The apostles are those who throw themselves into an unknown or desolate territory to open the way for the movement of God. The prophets are the forerunners, or those who announce and proclaim the direction of God's plans. Apostles, for their part, are the pioneers who put into work this word.

And God has appointed these in the church: first apostles, second prophets, third teachers, after that miracles, then gifts of healing . . . I Corinthians 12:28

The apostolic ministry is a pioneer ministry. Jesus, the apostle Paul, and Martin Luther were pioneers. The apostle is the first person to set foot in new territories. They open the way so that others may continue what God has started. They are the ones who reveal those truths that have been hidden or lost and for this reason are frequently persecuted and rejected.

For I think that God has displayed us, the apostles, last, as men condemned to death; for we have been made a spectacle to the world, both to angels and to men.

I Corinthians 4:9

Apostles are the spiritual architects as they establish the foundations upon which God can build His Church.

According to the grace of God which was given to me, as a wise master builder I have laid the foundation, and another builds on it. But let each one take heed how he builds on it. I Corinthians 3:10

We should understand that the extent of the apostolic calling must not to be considered with exaggerated importance. Although the Bible gives it a place of prominence, the apostolate, as much as the other ministerial roles, is given to imperfect human beings who are not infallible. It is a fact that neither apostles nor the new apostolic movement are perfect. Every apostle and every apostolic fountain simply represent a part of the universal body of Christ. The body consists of many members and all have an important contribution in accordance with their gift for the edification of the body.

If you desire to know more about the apostle's ministry, I recommend Dr. C. Peter Wagner's book, *Churchquake* (Wagner Publications, Colorado Springs, CO, 2000).

Apostles in the church

Therefore, holy brethren, partakers of the heavenly calling, consider the Apostle and High Priest of our confession, Christ Jesus. Hebrews 3:1

We find in the person of Christ the fullness of all the ministries. As God's envoy, Jesus is the perfect apostle. As for prophet, we find Him in Matthew 21:11; evangelist, Matthew 4:23; pastor, John 10:11; teacher, Matthew 23:8. Furthermore, with heavenly authority, Jesus chose twelve men, whom He named disciples and later commissioned as apostles.

> *And when it was day, He called His disciples to Him; and from them He chose twelve whom He also named apostles: Simon, whom He also named Peter, and Andrew his brother; James and John; Philip and Bartholomew; Matthew and Thomas; James the son of Alphaeus, and Simon called the Zealot; Judas the son of James, and Judas Iscariot who also became a traitor.* Luke 6:13–16

These are known as the twelve apostles of the Lamb. However, the Bible also mentions others as apostles, among them: Apollos (I Corinthians 4:6–9), Barnabas (Acts 14:3–4, 14), Epaphroditus (Philippians 2:25), Erastus (Acts 19:22), Junia (who was a woman, Romans 16:7), Matthias (Acts 1:26), Paul (Romans 11:13), James or Jacob (Acts 15:22), Timothy (1 Thessalonians 1:1, 2:6), Titus (II Corinthians 8:23) and others, whose names are not mentioned and who are messengers (*apostolos*, II Corinthians 8:23).

Women apostles?

Although I believe that this is a controversial issue, I simply desire to give an opinion based on the biblical context and pattern. It is not my intention to elaborate in relation to the ministry and authority of women, as there are entire books that have been written on this theme, some for and others against. I recommend the book *Women of Destiny* (Regal Publishers, 1999), written by Cindy Jacobs, as it presents clear arguments on this theme.

The culture of the Jewish people and the social conditions that prevailed in the times of Christ, together with the Aaronic priesthood, did not leave a place for women to be named as apostles. With the death of Christ, a form of government in the Church was restored that was similar to the standard of the judges, in which women could aspire to higher positions of authority.

> *Now Deborah, a prophetess, the wife of Lapidoth, was judging Israel at that time. And she would sit under the palm tree of Deborah between Ramah and Bethel in the mountains of Ephraim. And the children of Israel came up to her for judgment.* Judges 4:4–5

The Spirit Filled Life Bible notes, "*Deborah* demonstrates the possibilities for any woman today who will allow the Spirit of God to form and fill her life, developing her full capacities to shape the world around her."[1]

Historical and biblical reasons bring us to un-

1 *The Spirit Filled Life Bible*, (Thomas Nelson Publishers, Nashville, TN, 1991), p. 351.

derstand that the woman can take a governing position as apostle in the Church.

Phoebe (Romans 16:1) was recognized by Paul as *deaconess* of the church in Cenchrea, and a help (prostasis) to many. As Patricia Gundry points out, *prostasis* is a "supervisor" that indicates a position of high authority.[1]

Among the New Testament fathers of the Church we find various writings that affirm the feminine nature of Junia. In fact, in all the commentaries written about this text this is clearly recognized. Aegidos of Rome in the thirteenth century (1245–1316) was the first to say that Junia was a derivative of Andronicus, and consequently, a man.

John Chrysostom (337–407), bishop of Constantinople, was not partial to women. He wrote negatively about women, but he was very positive about Junia: "Oh, how great is the devotion of this woman who can be called worthy of the appellation of apostle!" He was not the only one of the Church fathers to believe that Junia was a woman. Origen of Alexandria (185–253) said that her name was a variation of Julia. Thayer's Lexicon cited Jerome (340–419), Hato of Vercelli (924–961), Theophylack (1058–1108), and Peter Abelard (1079–1142) all wrote of Junia as a woman.[2]

---

1 P. Gundry, *Women Can Be Free*, (Zondervan, 1977), p. 102.
2 Charles Trombley, *Who Said Women Can't Teach?*, (Bridge Publishing, 1985), p. 190–191. Taken from Cannistracci, *Apostles and the Emerging Apostolic Movement*, (Renew Books, 1996), p. 89.

We cannot pass over the fact that the apostle Paul, referring to the character and style of life of the apostles in their type of work, calls them tender and affectionate and compares them to a nurse who cares for her children. Undoubtedly, the feminine concepts were not an obstacle to identify his ministry and that of the apostles who accompanied him. The fact that Jesus did not choose women was already a given; the logic of their absence is like saying that no Latin American can be an apostle, prophet, or part of any other ministry because the Bible does not mention it. We ought to be careful about rejecting something simply because the Bible does not specifically mention it.

False apostles and prophets

> *I know your works, your labor, your patience, and that you cannot bear those who are evil. And you have tested those who say they are apostles and are not, and have found them liars.*　　　Revelation 2:2

> *Beloved, do not believe every spirit, but test the spirits, whether they are of God; because many false prophets have gone out into the world.*　　　I John 4:1

Those who insist on denying the ministries of the apostle and prophet due to the fact that the Bible warns us about the existence of false apostles and prophets do not realize the simple fact that the existence of false ones necessarily implies that true ones must also exist. If they misinterpret these passages, then we would have to assume that neither pastors, teachers, evangelists, nor even Christ exist, as the Bible also speaks of false pastors (John 10:12–13), teachers (II Peter 2:1), evangelists (Galatians 1:9), brethren (Galatians 2:4), and even false Christs (Mark 13:22).[1]

> *Therefore we who are called to be and who are now apostles need to concentrate on serving and ministering to the saints, upholding and edifying them into the building that God wants them to be. Remember, the apostles and prophets are not the roof and pinnacle on top of the building but the foundation at the bottom of the building. We are not to lord it over the saints and other ministers but remain the apostle-prophet foundation that supports the Church.[2]*

1 Cannistracci, *Apostles and the Emerging Apostolic Movement*, (Renew Books, 1996), p. 19.
2 Dr. Bill Hamon, *Apostles, Prophets and the Coming Moves of God*, (Destiny Image Publishers, 1997), p. 220.

9

Spiritual Pioneers

By John Eckhardt

The author is recognized as an apostle and expert in the area of national church leadership. He supervises and directs Crusaders Ministries in Chicago, Illinois. He travels throughout the world teaching biblical truths of the apostolic and prophetic church and the ministries of the apostle and prophet. He is the author of fourteen publications and produces daily radio and television programs.

One of the characteristics of apostles is that they are spiritual pioneers. Martin Luther was a pioneer. The apostle Paul was a pioneer: he opened new paths. Apostles are fleeting runners: they open a path for others to continue. The apostles are the first to go into a new territory and frequently usher in a new truth. They will surely be misunderstood simply because they go out and speak first.

Consequently, apostles are frequently resisted and persecuted. Pioneers are generally considered to be odd and at times crazy. Apostles are attacked for the truth they preach and what they present that appears completely new to the Church.

And God has appointed these in the church: first apostles, second prophets, third teachers, after that miracles, then gifts of healings, helps, administrations, varieties of tongues.   1 Corinthians 12:28

For I think that God has displayed us, the apostles, last, as men condemned to death; for we have been made a spectacle to the world, both to angels and to men.
                              1 Corinthians 4:9

Though the apostles were placed first in the church, they are generally treated as last. The Greek word which translates as "first" is *proton*, which denotes first in time, place or importance. It also means at first, principle, first of all and before. Apostles are pathfinders. A pathfinder is one who discovers a way, especially one who explores untraversed regions to mark out a new route. Pioneers are the first to enter a new region. This can be a new region geographically or a new region of knowledge.

Pioneers leave a heritage for others to follow. They leave a spiritual legacy for those who will come after them. This ministry precedes and opens the way for others. The early apostles left a spiritual legacy for the Church to follow. We all have inherited the spiritual legacy of the early apostles.

Apostolic power has the ability to penetrate new areas and regions and to make a clear way for others to follow. Apostles ought to be able to break through spiritual obstacles that keep people from advancing. To be a pioneer means to start or take part in the development of something new.

Spiritual Architects—Master Builders

According to the grace of God which was given to me, as a wise master builder I have laid the foundation, and another builds on it. But let each one take heed how he builds on it.   1 Corinthians 3:10

The expression "wise master builder" alludes to an architect. An architect is a person who designs buildings and supervises their construction. What concerns the apostles is designing, structuring, and forming. When there is reform, the Church ought to be redesigned and restructured. Structures are built after they are designed. This applies both to that which is natural and to that which is spiritual.

When beginning a structure, the first thing that is placed is the foundation. In such a way, apostles lay the foundation and are the support of the structure. The Church is a spiritual structure. The Church is designed to be the building of God. To build means to construct. From here comes our word building.

If we are not building the Church in conformity with the Lord's model, the apostles will discern and know it. They will know when things are out of order. Just as architects advise builders when they have left the original design, in the same way, apostles know when the Church has departed from

God's original plan. Once the foundations have been laid, the apostles will supervise how the spiritual building is being constructed.

The foundation of Martin's Luther reform was justification by faith. Luther received and began to preach that believers are justified by faith and not through works. The Church had to be reconstructed upon this doctrinal foundation. Even so, together with the preaching and teaching of the doctrine of salvation by faith, preachers had to be trained. In the same way, the churches had to be organized and governed under a new plan. It is not enough just to lay the foundation. The building must be constructed upon it.

Many of Luther's followers did not have the wisdom to build upon the foundation of faith. Luther had to correct and even disassociate with others who took a mistaken direction with the reform. This does not mean that Luther was correct in all this theology, but the apostolic anointing upon his life gave him a vision to build the Church after the foundation was laid.

When the Church is reformed, those will arise who have the anointing to govern it. The word governing found in 1 Corinthians 12:28 comes from the Greek term *kubernesis*, which signifies driving or piloting. The ability to drive a church through its correct course is given to the Church through governing anointing. Without this anointing, those who lead the Church will take it off the correct course. The apostles ought to guard the Church from every wind of doctrinal error. Those who govern are necessary to keep the Church on the track of true reform.

Spiritual Frontiers

A frontier is a new field for developmental activity, a region that forms the margin of settled or developed territory. We call this "living on the cutting edge." Frontiersmen live, obviously, on the frontier. They are on the front line. The apostolic anointing will keep the Church on the cutting edge. Apostles are spiritual frontiersmen. They live and minister on the frontier. Just as there are natural frontiers, there are also spiritual frontiers.

Often the frontier is in a specific place, and the Lord continues to send apostles to expand the Church. They are sent to new regions geographically as well as spiritually. They expand our spiritual horizons and release us from spiritual boundaries and limitations of tradition and past experience.

There is a song that we sing in our church, written by my good friend Kevin Leal. Following are the words to the chorus:

> *Opening places in the spirit*
> *where men have never been.*
> *Opening places in the spirit*
> *so He can come again.*
> *Opening places in the spirit*
> *letting men break through.*

Opening places in the spirit
touching you and you and you!

These are new places in the spirit that need to be opened and where many saints have never been. It takes the anointing to open those places for others to follow and enter in. These are the individuals and churches that will operate in apostolic anointing to open new regions and new frontiers so that others may enter in and experience the fullness of God.

This agrees with the fact that the apostolic unction is a pioneering anointing. Pioneers are the first (*proton*) to enter a new place with a new truth. As the first, they are situated in a special and important place. Those who leave behind a spiritual legacy will always have a special place for those who follow. Additionally, the word last comes from the Greek *eschatos* which means "the lowest." Because this ministry does much damage to the kingdom of darkness, it is the most persecuted and attacked by the enemy.

Paul says that this ministry has been "made a spectacle." The Greek term that translates into spectacle is *theatron,* from which our word theater is derived. This means that the apostolic ministry is about a scene that the world, the Church, and the angels want to see. Nonetheless, apostles are often treated like the dregs of society.

Even to the present hour we both hunger and thirst,
and we are poorly clothed, and beaten, and homeless.

128

And we labor, working with our own hands. Being reviled, we bless; being persecuted, we endure it; being defamed, we entreat. We have been made as the filth of the world, the offscouring of all things until now.

1 Corinthians 4:11–13

According to this description of the apostolic ministry from Paul himself, the apostles are beaten, humiliated, and discredited. This is the way many people react when confronted with the ministry of an apostle.

Furthermore, the word "filth" signifies offscouring. In other words, the apostles many times are treated like leftovers. Why is it that a ministry that the Lord says is the first is often treated like the last?

The answer is that the apostles are precursors and spiritual pioneers. Precursors and pioneers are almost always misunderstood and mistreated. It is not easy to open up new paths. When you study the lives of apostolic reformers you discover that they were hated and treated poorly by the religious system of their day. Any ministry that causes ruin to the kingdom of Satan can assume that it will be attacked.

Due to the lack of knowledge that the Church has had in relation to the apostle's ministry, it has been opposed to it as well on many occasions.

Apostolic Grace

One part of the grace given to apostles is the ability to withstand the persecution and opposition that come against this office. It would be crazy to exercise this office without the necessary grace.

Whoever understands the intense persecution that apostles face would never dare use the title or exercise the office of apostle without the firm conviction of being called and anointed to do so. Grace provides the ability to walk and act out whatever duty is necessary, despite persecution and lack of understanding.

As forerunners and pioneers, apostles are often rejected, misunderstood, and persecuted. But the grace that flows over them will make them successful in their mission.

> *And the word of the Lord was being spread throughout all the region.*   Acts 13:49

> *To preach the gospel in the regions beyond you, and not to boast in another man's sphere of accomplishment.*
>   2 Corinthians 10:16

Some Christians believe their cities already have enough churches, and they need to revive the existing ones rather than build new ones. But many of the existing churches will not receive new things, often fighting against a fresh move of the Holy Spirit. As a result, many of the present churches are ineffective. This is why I do not focus on the number of churches in an area, but on the number of churches having an *impact*. Often the number ranges from few to almost none. This is why apostolic ministry is needed: to plant effective, powerful churches that will have an impact!

Before a region opens to the gospel, however, the strongman of Matthew 12:29 must first be bound. (See also Mark 3:27; Luke 11:21,22.) The strongman may in fact be a demonic principality that rules over a certain geographical area, leading a horde of demonic principalities that influence the affairs of people. The Bible clearly demonstrates God's superiority over all the "principalities and powers." (Compare Daniel 7–10 with Ephesians 1:21 and 6:12, Colossians 1:16 and Romans 8:38, where the Messiah decisively defeats all His enemies.) The "goods" are the souls that are being influenced and controlled, by this ruling spirit, to keep them from the truth. Apostles can go into new regions and break through the resistance by binding the strongman.

The strongman is bound by the overall ministry of the apostle. The apostle then establishes new churches and new revelation in these areas. Even where there are already churches in existence, an apostle can come in and establish new revelation. Often the strongmen in these areas are spirits of religion and tradition.

The apostle Paul had the desire to preach the gospel and to establish churches in new regions. He did not desire to boast in another man's work, but to preach Christ where He had not been preached.

*And the next Sabbath almost the whole city came to-
gether to hear the word of God.*　　　　Acts 13:44

In addition to regions being opened up to the
Word of God, the Lord uses apostles to affect cities
as well. Remember, some are called to cities, some to
regions and some to nations. Those called to certain
cities will be commissioned to establish the truth in
that city. This does not mean that every church in
that city comes under an apostle's authority. The
apostle has authority only in the place where he
ministers or is allowed to minister.

The Lord is now raising up apostles who will
be voices in major cities. Wherever God sends His
apostles, they will help change the spiritual climate
of their assigned areas, whether those areas are cities, regions or nations. The result will be that the
people in those areas are more receptive to hearing
the Word of God—and the Church will be that much
closer to fulfilling its mission.

Church Planters

I planted, Apollos watered, but God gave the increase.
1 Corinthians 3:6

Apostles are sowers. Planters establish doctrine
and churches. Where there is no growth, planting is
necessary. Paul was a planter. He went to new areas
as a pioneer and planted new churches.

Planting is important for replacing. When churches die, other new ones should be planted. There are many churches that, at one time, had the fire of God but now are dying. This can be the result of tradition or because the form or content of worship is not impacting the present generation. You cannot sing songs from 1850 to a generation from the twenty-first century. Many denominations that were born years ago have lost their impact on the new generation. The Lord raises apostles to sow new works and reach new generations.

10

Warfare

By John Eckhardt

For the weapons of our warfare are not carnal but mighty in God for pulling down strongholds, casting down arguments and every high thing that exalts itself against the knowledge of God, bringing every thought into captivity to the obedience of Christ. 2 Corinthians 10:4–5

Many Christians are familiar with these verses in 2 Corinthians, and some are actively involved in practicing them. Yet countless Christians lament their ineffectiveness when it comes to seeing results in the area of spiritual warfare. Why is that?

The commission given to the Church requires us to invade new territories—hostile territories. The powers of darkness that have ruled regions for centuries will not give up without a fight. They must be confronted, subdued, and driven out. This requires warfare.

Many do not understand the present-day emphasis in the Church on spiritual warfare. Some even oppose the very thought of it. But opposition notwithstanding, there is a growing emphasis today on warfare prayer. Dr. C. Peter Wagner of Global Harvest Ministries in Colorado has written some excellent books on warfare prayer called the *Prayer Warrior Series*, published by Regal Books, as well as *Pulling Down Strongholds*, by Hector P. Torres, Wagner Publications. I recommend these books highly to every pastor and intercessor who wants a better understanding of this important subject.

Warfare is nothing new. The Bible is filled with warfare. Apostles and apostolic people will be a people of warfare, whether they use the term or not.

Pulling Down Strongholds

Warfare in 2 Corinthians 10:4 is translated from the Greek word *strateia*, meaning apostolic, career, military service (as one of hardship and danger). It is related to the Greek word *strateuomai*, meaning to execute the *apostolate* (with its arduous duties and functions) and to contend with carnal thoughts. Paul was saying that the weapons of his apostolic ministry were mighty for the pulling down of strongholds.

I am convinced that there are certain strongholds that cannot be destroyed without the apostolic anointing. "Stronghold" is the Greek word *ochuroma*, meaning a fortress, a castle, a fortified place. Satan and his demons have fortified themselves from invasion. They have built strongholds and fortified themselves in every region of the world to resist the advancement of the Kingdom. These strongholds must be dealt with if we are to see the fulfillment of the Great Commission. Apostles have the ability to confront and pull down these strongholds.

The apostle Paul links these strongholds with "imaginations." This is the Greek word *logismos*, meaning reasoning, thought, computation, or logic. It carries the idea of holding something safely. It is simply the way people think based on their way of life, tradition, experience, or past teaching. Unfortunately, most thinking is against the knowledge of God.

The stronghold is also made up of demonic influence. There is a wisdom that is earthly, sensual, and devilish (see Jas. 3:15). *Logismos* can also be translated as "arguments." Strongholds are the mind-sets of people in a particular territory. These mind-sets are fortified places that keep out truth and hold in lies. Unbelievers have mind-sets that prevent them from receiving the truth of the gospel. Spiritual warfare involves demolishing these mind-sets so that people can receive and walk in the truth.

Dr. Clarence Walker defines a stronghold as a forceful, stubborn argument, rationale, opinion, idea and/or philosophy that is formed and resists the knowledge of Jesus Christ. The *Twentieth Century New Testament* translation says, "We are engaged in confuting arguments and pulling down every barrier raised against the knowledge of God." Strongholds do two things: They keep people from the knowledge of God, and they prevent people from obeying the truth. Ignorance and rebellion are the result.

The term *mind-set* is a combination of both mind and set. In other words, the mind is already settled on a set of beliefs, and therefore resists change. This means it is fixed and rigid. Most people who claim to be open-minded really are not. Their minds are closed and hardened to truth and revelation.

Mind-sets are thought processes of people groups who have developed a way of thinking over centuries of time. It is a combination of their experiences and what they have been taught by their ancestors. Mind-sets are not easy to change. It takes a strong anointing to break through the defensive barriers in their minds and overcome the pride associated with their ways of thinking.

People are proud of the way they think, even though it may be wrong. No one wants to admit they are wrong, particularly when their ancestors have thought a certain way for sometimes thousands of years. Humility must precede repentance, and pride will put up a fight.

These strongholds are so strong that they are likened to forts. A fort is a citadel, a garrison, a castle, a tower, a safeguard. We have all heard the saying, "Hold the fort!" It means to defend and maintain the status quo. People would rather maintain their present way of thinking than to change. They will defend the current way of thinking through argument and debate. They will contradict and even blaspheme if necessary.

Communism is a mind-set; it is an ideology and

philosophy of life. Materialism is a mind-set that bases happiness on success. Islam is a mind-set. Hinduism is a mind-set. These philosophies control the minds of countless people. They are powerful strongholds that can only be overcome through apostolic preaching and teaching.

Strongholds are major hindrances to the advancing of the Church and must be dealt with apostolically. The preaching, teaching, and overall ministry of apostolic people are weapons that are mighty through God for the pulling down of these strongholds. (Praise, worship, and prayer also are effective weapons.) The first thing Jesus gave the Twelve when He sent them forth was power over devils (see Matt. 10:1).

The Church must have the ability to blast and demolish these fortresses. Apostolic ministry has the power and authority to destroy strongholds and change mind-sets. There is a grace, a supernatural ability to refute, disprove, discredit and expose these philosophies for what they are. People will not repent unless there is a change of mind. This is the warfare that the apostle Paul is referring to in 2 Corinthians 10:3–5—refuting arguments and taking captive philosophies that are contrary to the truth.

Greek Spirits

The Greek world in which the early apostles ministered was filled with such philosophies. The Greeks were lovers of wisdom. They were seekers of knowledge to the point of being guilty of mind idolatry. In other words, they worshipped knowledge. They were the guardians of Aristotle and Plato and countless other philosophers. They had strong opinions and defended their point of view. They took pleasure in arguing and debating.

It was into this kind of world that the Church was birthed. It would have been impossible for the Church to succeed in its mission there without the grace of God. The apostolic grace and anointing upon the Early Church gave them the ability to challenge and overcome these strongholds.

We find these same spirits operating on many college campuses today. They are strongholds of intellectualism and rationalization. It is no coincidence that members of fraternities and sororities are called "Greeks." As I was traveling through a college town, the Spirit of the Lord drew my attention to the fraternity houses on the campus. As I looked at all of the Greek letters that identified the different fraternities and sororities, the words "Greek Spirits" came into my spirit. As I meditated upon what the Holy Spirit gave me, I began to understand the kind of spirits that the early apostles encountered.

The world in their day was controlled politically by the Romans, but influenced culturally by the Greeks. Philosophy was a major stronghold. Spirits of intellectualism and rationalization prevented many from believing that Christ had risen from the dead. College campuses are filled with these kinds of spirits.

Spirits of intellectualism, rationalization, pride, debate, and mind idolatry are ruling spirits that the early apostles dealt with. Just as they were able to break through the arguments of pagan philosophy, so must we.

The *New English Bible* says, "We demolish sophistries and all that rears its proud head against the knowledge of God" (2 Cor. 10:5). Sophists were Greek philosophers who specialized in dialectic argumentation and rhetoric. They were professional philosophers and teachers skilled in elaborate and devious argumentation. Sophism today is defined as plausible but fallacious argument. In other words, it is deceptive. At the root of deceptive philosophy is the devil himself.

The Jews sought after a sign, and the Greeks sought after wisdom (see 1 Cor. 1:22). The Greeks, however, were not seeking after the wisdom of God. They were seeking after philosophy. Many viewed Christianity as just another philosophy open to debate. The Phillips translation calls the type of wisdom sought by the Greeks "an intellectual panacea." They viewed philosophy and education as a cure-all. But we preach Christ crucified—to the Jews a stumbling block, to the Greeks foolishness (see 1 Cor. 1:23). The Greeks considered the preaching of the Cross to be nonsense.

It was into this pagan, Greek, philosophical

world that the Early Church was thrust. They were carriers of an anointing that was able to pull down these strongholds. At the root of Greek philosophy was pride. The Greeks were proud of their philosophical heritage and argued when confronted with the truth of the gospel. Apostolic ministry confounds the philosophies of men. It is a ministry of power that breaks through the arguments that Satan has set up in the minds of men.

God uses this ministry to make foolish the wisdom of this world (see 1 Cor. 1:20). We need this same kind of ministry today to confront the arguments that our modern world raises against the truth. Although the arguments may have changed, the demonic influence behind them has not. We are dealing with ancient principalities that must be bound and cast out through apostolic ministry. These are stubborn arguments that refuse to budge; they can only be destroyed through apostolic ministry, an anointing that confounds the wisdom of this world and releases the wisdom of God.

The Church needs apostolic grace today to refute the arguments that people in our modern world use to reject the gospel. Miracles, healing, signs, and wonders help to blast away these strongholds. People have no argument against the raw power of God. They have a difficult time explaining these things away. They are forced to rethink their positions and come face-to-face with the truth. Apostles come, not with enticing words of man's wisdom, but in demonstration of the Spirit and of power.

This is again why the Church must be, first and foremost, apostolic. Without this dimension, we will not have the ability to destroy these strongholds. We are not just dealing with views but *worldviews*. Entire people groups think certain ways. Entire segments of the world think certain ways. Without the apostolic anointing, how can we succeed against these pervasive worldviews? How can we, without the apostolic anointing, free the millions of people from mind-sets that will send them to eternal damnation?

The Apostle's Mantle

According to Dr. Paula A. Price in *God's Apostle Revived*,[1] the apostle's mantle includes warfare strategy and rulership.

As mentioned earlier, the Greek word *strateia* means military service or apostolic career. The kin term *strateuomai* means to serve in a military campaign, to execute the *apostolate*. This word's definition speaks of armaments, troops and battle array. According to Dr. Price, the apostle surfaces as an "arch warrior, a chief strategist, a competent captain, and an able guard over his jurisdiction." His supernatural rank in the *stratos* makes him a formidable

1 Paula A. Price, *God's Apostle Revived* (Everlasting Life Publications: Plainfield, New Jersey, 1994).

combatant in the spirit realm and an arch rival to the forces in the heavenlies.

Indeed I have given him as a witness to the people, a leader and commander for the people.   Isaiah 55:4

Although every believer has rank to cast out devils, apostles walk and minister in the highest rank. Evil spirits and angels recognize this rank. Apostles are the spiritual commanders of the Church. "Commander," as used in Isaiah 55:4, is the Hebrew word *tsavah,* meaning to command, send a message, to put or set in order. The Church needs apostles to help set it in order. They help organize and mobilize the believers into an army.

Apostles are standard-bearers—commanders who lift the standard and rally the army of God (see Isa. 59:19). An apostolic church is a church that is awesome or terrible, as an army with banners (see Song of Sol. 6:4,10). Apostolic churches strike fear into the kingdom of darkness.

Apostles have the ability as generals and commanders to mobilize the saints for war. Apostles rally the people of God. To rally means to bring order again, to gather and organize anew. It is the ability to draw people together for action. Apostles are given the rank and authority to do this. They are leaders with the necessary grace, charisma, and wisdom to lead the Church.

Apostolic Churches Strike Fear into the Kingdom of Darkness

Apostolic ministry is a ministry of warfare. It entails commanding, mobilizing, rallying, and gathering the army of God to challenge and pull down the strongholds of the enemy. The apostolic invades new territories and breaks through. It has the ability to go first. It is the first to encounter the spiritual resistance of the powers of darkness and the first to penetrate the barriers they erect. This ministry is absolutely necessary to keep the Church advancing toward the completion of the Great Commission.

The Ravenous Bird

Declaring the end from the beginning, and from ancient times things are not yet done, saying, "My counsel shall stand, and I will do all My pleasure," calling a [ravenous] bird of prey from the east, the man who executes My counsel, from a far country. Indeed I have spoken it; I will also bring it to pass. I have purposed it; I will also do it. Isaiah 46:10,11

God has a plan and purpose He will fulfill. It has already been spoken by the prophets. Nothing will stand in the way of His fulfilling His good pleasure; His counsel shall stand. We have the glorious opportunity to be a part of this plan. As we discover the plan of God, we pray and align ourselves with His will. We are laborers together with God.

God calls the ravenous bird of prey to execute His purposes. This is a prophetic symbol of the apostolic ministry. The ravenous bird is the Hebrew word *ayit,* meaning a hawk. It also means to swoop down upon. The hawk is a symbol of war, representing the militaristic aspect of the apostle.

Another contemporary definition for "hawk" is one who demonstrates an actively aggressive or combative attitude. It is a person who favors military force or action in order to carry out a foreign policy. What a symbol for the apostolic!

The Church also has a foreign policy. We are commissioned to go into all the world and preach the gospel. We must have an aggressive, warlike attitude against the forces of darkness that would attempt to stop us.

The hawk symbolizes sharpness, keen vision, and quickness. It represents discernment and insight into the plans and purposes of God. The hawk is a swift bird that suddenly seizes its prey. It is a ravenous bird. Ravenous means extremely hungry, voracious, or greedy for gratification. This bird symbolizes the militant, aggressive, and warlike aspect of the apostolic ministry. It is needed to execute the plans of God.

As an officer in the Church, the apostle is also an executive. He is a person who executes power in the Church. In other words, he has the power and authority to execute the plans and purposes of God. To execute means to put into effect, to carry out, to perform, to fulfill, to finish. The purposes of God will not be fulfilled or carried out without the apostolic ministry being restored to the Church.

For too long the Church has tried to carry out the plan of God while ignoring the vital ministry. God calls the ravenous bird to execute His counsel. These are military generals and commanders who will mobilize the people of God for the fulfillment of God's purposes. They have an appetite and an authority to execute. We need people who do more than talk and sing. They must *do* and *act*. They have the ability to finish and complete the commissions given to them by the Lord.

The apostolic Church must be quick in executing the plans of the Lord. The hawk moves swiftly; it does not take long to swoop down and devour its prey. The Church in the book of Acts experienced rapid movement, achieving tremendous breakthroughs in a short period of time. The move of God accelerated and gained momentum from Jerusalem on the day of Pentecost. Large numbers of believers were added to the Church quickly. This is the kind of anointing the Church will need in the last days to fulfill the Great Commission. There is much work to be done in a short period. The Lord desires to do a quick work.

Prayer and the Apostolic

> *Therefore pray the Lord of the harvest to send out laborers into His harvest.* Matthew 9:38

We are living in the midst of the greatest prayer revival the world has ever known. More people are praying for revival and global evangelism than ever before. Recent breakthroughs in the 10/40 window—the geographical area between 10th and 40th parallel north of the equator, ranging from west Africa to the Far East—have been attributed to this recent prayer movement. Prayer teams are visiting remote and isolated places to pray for the fulfillment of the Great Commission. Gateway cities are being targeted for prayer in nations with little or no Christian presence. God is stirring His people to pray around the world. What is happening? Is this the sign that we may be nearing the final thrust in world evangelization? I believe the answer is *yes*.

The worldwide prayer movement is releasing an apostolic spirit upon the Church. This is because prayer releases the apostolic anointing. Jesus encouraged us to pray to the Lord to send forth laborers into His harvest (see Luke 10:2). Remember, *send forth* is an apostolic term. This shows us the connection between prayer and the apostolic.

The apostolic revolves around the concept of sending and being sent. God has always been a *sending* God. He sent Moses into Egypt when He heard the cries of His people in bondage. He continually sent prophets to Israel to warn them of the consequences of their rebellion. He sent John the Baptist to prepare the way of the Lord. He sent His only begotten Son to die for the sins of the world. He sent the Holy Spirit to help us and to be our Comforter. The apostolic spirit is a part of the vary nature of God.

Our prayers move God. He responds to our prayers by sending forth His Spirit. He sends laborers as a result of our prayers. This is why the Lord encourages us to pray. Every nation needs "sent ones." The harvest is plenteous, but the laborers are few. The world needs apostolic laborers to bring in the harvest.

I believe that, in response to the millions who are currently praying, more apostles and apostolic ministries will be released in this hour than ever before. In fact, I believe the greatest apostolic spirit the world has ever known is even now beginning to be released. It will be greater than what we read of in the book of Acts. The coming move of God will dwarf the acts of apostles by comparison. It is already happening. The largest churches the world has ever known are now on the earth. There are more Christians alive today than at any other time in history. There are more miracles and healings taking place than ever before. There are more apostles and prophets on the earth than ever before. We are living in apostolic times.

Apostolic Times

> *Behold, you despisers, marvel and perish! For I work a work in your days, a work which you will by no means believe, though one were to declare it to you.*
>
> Acts 13:41

*Look among the nations and watch—Be utterly as-
tounded! For I will work a work in your days which
you would not believe, though it were told you.*

Habbakkuk 1:5

Paul quoted the prophecy of Habakkuk in describing what was taking place in the book of Acts.
It was a warning to the Jews who would not believe
the numbers of Gentiles that God would receive by
their faith. It was something so new and awesome
that there was a danger of despising it. Habakkuk
told them to look out among the heathen and won-
der. God was about to do something in the nations
of the world that would be unbelievable.

This verse describes what takes place during
apostolic times. No one would doubt that the book
of Acts describes what took place during apostolic
times. What Habakkuk stated, however, can happen
at any time—and it is happening today. God is
working in the nations of the world. We are looking
out among the nations and seeing things that we
may not have believed several years ago. This is
why I say we are now living in apostolic times.

Apostolic times are seasons in which God releases and apostolic spirit to the Church. God begins
to raise up apostolic leaders and apostolic churches.
This is always in response to prayer, and this is what
is happening today. Apostles are being positioned
in every nation to reap an end-times harvest.

Praying with Power

> *Now it came to pass in those days that He went out to the mountain to pray, and continued all night in prayer to God. And when it was day, He called His disciples to Himself; and from them He chose twelve whom He also named apostles.* Luke 6:12,13

Notice Jesus prayed all night before choosing the Twelve. Again, prayer releases the apostolic. I encourage churches to pray for their cities and nations to release an apostolic spirit into that region. Our local church in Chicago has emphasized all-night prayer to release the apostolic spirit into our own region. All-night prayer is a powerful way to release the apostolic spirit.

As we pray, apostles can be identified and released into every region. We need to identify the true apostles in a region. They may not be the ones *we* would identify; we need to know whom *God* identifies. A well-known preacher may not be the one. Sometimes those whom God chooses are hidden until prayer releases them.

Prayer not only releases the apostolic spirit; it sustains an apostolic movement. Prayer releases spiritual impetus and momentum. The Church in the book of Acts was a praying church. They continued to break through in spite of resistance, persecution, even death. They prayed until "the place where they were assembled together was shaken" (Acts

4:31). The result of their praying was an apostolic release of great power and great grace (see v. 33). Signs and wonders were released, and "believers were increasingly added to the Lord" (Acts 5:14). The apostolic spirit that is released through prayer fuels church growth; it is a harvest anointing.

The apostles gave themselves continually to prayer (see Acts 6:4). Prayer is the strength of the apostolic ministry. Apostolic churches are being raised up throughout the earth that will be houses of prayer for all nations (see Isa. 56:7); then we can ask God for the nations (see Ps. 2:8).

Because of the authority and power resident within the apostolic anointing, greater results take place when we pray apostolically. Many have heard of prophetic prayer, but few have heard of apostolic prayer.

Apostolic prayer is strategic prayer. It is a governmental praying. It is global in perspective, with a wisdom to fulfill God's end-times purposes. This is because apostles, along with prophets, bring revelation to the Church to fulfill the plans and purposes of the Lord. They give us insight into the eternal purposes of God. Those who come into contact with true apostles gain a better understanding of God's purposes as revealed in the Word of God.

Apostolic prayer is revelational. Apostolic people pray with the advantage of the wisdom of God. It is praying with the authority that comes from revelation. We are praying things today that we never prayed five years ago. This is because we are seeing things in the Word we never saw before. As a result, our prayers are stronger and deeper than ever before.

Apostolic prayer is warfare prayer. Epaphras labored fervently in prayer for the Colossian church (see Col. 4:12). *Laboring* is an apostolic term. It is the Greek word *agonizomia,* meaning to struggle or contend with an adversary, to strive. Apostles and apostolic people contend with the powers of darkness in prayer. Apostolic prayer breaks the resistance in regions that have been held captive by the powers of darkness. This type of intercession will help believers stand perfect and complete in all the will of God.

Apostolic prayer is unceasing (see 1 Thess. 5:17). It does not rest until the plans and purposes of God are complete. The apostolic ministry is tenacious and relentless in its drive to finish. It does not cease because of resistance or temporary setbacks. It continues to pioneer and break through every barrier until the commission is fulfilled. This is another reason Satan hates and fears this anointing. It is an unstoppable force. It is persistent and patient in spite of trials and tribulations. It is a battering ram against the citadels of darkness.

The Antioch Principle

Now in the church that was at Antioch there were certain prophets and teachers: Barnabas, Simeon who was called Niger, Lucius of Cyrene, Manaen who had been brought up with Herod the tetrarch, and Saul. As they ministered to the Lord and fasted, the Holy Spirit said, "Now separate to Me Barnabas and Saul for the work to which I have called them."

Then, having fasted and prayed, and laid hands on them, they sent them away. So, being sent out by the Holy Spirit, they went down to Seleucia, and from there they sailed to Cyprus. Acts 13:1–4

Apostolic times are times in which the apostolic spirit and the apostolic ministry are being released. This can be done through prayer; it is happening today. There is, however, another way to release the apostolic. I call this the "Antioch principle." It is based on what happened in the church at Antioch. As the prophets and teachers came together to minister to the Lord and fast, the Holy Ghost said, "Separate to Me Barnabas and Saul." They were separated for an apostolic ministry. Ministering to the Lord and fasting helped release them into their ministries.

There is also in these verses a prophetic element for the Church today. The Scripture identifies prophets and teachers coming together to minister to the Lord and to fast. I believe this represents the two movements that preceded this present apostolic move. The Church has already seen a release of the teaching anointing and the prophetic anointing. It is important that these two movements come together to help release the apostolic anointing. Prophets and teachers should not fight apostles, but rather be a part of releasing them. Some of the prophets and teachers themselves will be released into apostolic ministries.

Fasting, along with prayer, is a way of releasing apostles. After the church of Antioch fasted and prayed, they sent Barnabas and Saul away. These two apostles were released through fasting and praying. They were then sent forth by the Holy Spirit.

A Finishing Anointing

Jesus said to them, "My food is to do the will of Him who sent Me, and to finish His work."   John 4:34

Notice the two words "sent" and "finish." Jesus was *sent* by the Father, and His desire was to *finish* His mission. This verse connects being sent with finishing. This is why I call the apostolic anointing a "finishing anointing." It will take an apostolic Church to finish the Great Commission. To finish not only means to reach the end of a task or course, it means something that completes, concludes or perfects.

The Lord is preparing the Church to complete its task, and the apostolic ministry is absolutely essential to prepare the Church for this purpose. Without the ministry of the apostle, the Church will lack the necessary grace, power, and authority to finish or complete its mission.

> *And see, now I go bound in the spirit to Jerusalem, not knowing the things that will happen to me there, except that the Holy Spirit testifies in every city, saying that chains and tribulations await me.*
>
> *But none of these things move me; nor do I count my life dear to myself, so that I may finish my race with joy, and the ministry which I received from the Lord Jesus, to testify to the gospel of the grace of God.*
>
> Acts 20:22–24

Notice Paul's attitude. He was determined to finish his course. Nothing could dissuade him from completing his ministry. There was a drive and a determination to finish. This must be the mind-set of the Church today. We must have an apostolic mind-set; we must be driven and determined to complete all obstacles and hindrances that stand in the way of finishing.

Trials, tests, and tribulations do not deter the true apostolic ministry. There is a grace resident within this anointing that overcomes all opposition and breaks through every barrier. And it does not cease until the task is complete.

11

Hitching Apostles to Prophets

From the book *Apostles and Prophets,
Foundation of the Church*, Regal Publishers.

By Dr. C. Peter Wagner

*Dr. Wagner is recognized as the overseen Apostle for the Apostolic
Council of Prophetic Elders. He is the Director and founder of the
Wagner Institute for Practical Ministry in Colorado Springs, CO. He
is the cofounder of the World Prayer Center, in the same city and is a
recognized authority in the topics of Church Growth, Prayer and The
New Apostolic Reformation. He is the author of numerous books. He
and his wife reside in Colorado Springs.*

I love the analogy of apostles being "hitched" to prophets like two fine draft horses are hitched to each other. Both Doris and I are dairy farmers with roots in rural upstate New York. We both lived on farms in the 1930s when draft horses were standard farm equipment. I can remember driving a team on our hay wagon when I was five years old. We had no tractor in those days.

This explains why Doris and I like to go to live-stock shows where our favorite event is the draft horse competition. We love to see those magnificent Percherons and Clydesdales and Belgians and Shires working together as teams. The climax of all is the horse pull in which a team of two horses weighing 4,500 lbs. between them will often pull 14,000 lbs. of concrete blocks on a flat sled. I remember one county fair that featured individual horse pulls. The winner pulled 5,000 lbs. and the runner up pulled 4,000 lbs. But hitched together, they pulled 13,000 lbs.!

What does this say about apostles and prophets? Apostles can do certain good things on their own. Prophets can do certain good things on their own, but hitched together, they can change the world! I want to explain how this can happen in real life.

Pulling Together

Many draft horse breeders take their teams from show to show on a circuit, so the same teams will compete against each other more than once. It is not unusual to see one team beat another in one show, and then be beaten by the other in the next show. What is the variable? The horses which pull together on a given day win. The central figure is the 180 lb. teamster holding the reins and controlling more than two tons of horse flesh. When the team is hitched to the sled, the audience becomes absolutely silent. The horses are coiled like springs, trembling and stepping around in place with pent up nervous energy. Suddenly the teamster shouts "Giddap!" and the horses are off! If the teamster shouts at the split second when they are both moving forward together, they win. If they are not moving in the same direction at that moment, the strongest team in the show will lose. It's as simple as that.

This is the same with apostles and prophets. Sadly, many authentic apostles and prophets are losers. They do a little, all of which may be good, but they never reach their God-given potential because they are not pulling together.

On the other hand, those apostles and prophets who are winners have come to understand and appreciate their mutual roles in the kingdom of God. They know how to relate to one another in a positive way. They constantly add value to each other. As Bill Hamon would say, they are totally interdependent.

There are at least two ways, both found in the New Testament, that apostles and prophets relate to each other:

- **A casual relationship.** Sometimes a prophet and an apostle will find themselves meeting together at a given time, and the prophet might have a word from God to speak into the apostle. This has happened to me frequently. In the New Testament, the relationship that Paul had to Agabus illustrates the point (see Acts 21:10–13). I like to refer to this as a "Paul-Agabus" relationship. Paul and Agabus did not have an ongoing relationship, simply a casual one.

- **A structured relationship.** In this case the apostle and the prophet have placed themselves in a position to communicate with each other on a regular, ongoing basis. The relationship can be so close that their normal modus operandi is never to enter into important ministry activities without the participation or at least the knowledge of the other. The apostle Paul, who brought the prophet Silas into his core ministry team, models this for us (see Acts 15:40). This "Paul-Silas" relationship could been seen as the two being "harnessed" together, while the "Paul-Agabus" relationship would see them as being "tied" together.

My apostolic relationship with Prophet Chuck Pierce is a current example of a Paul-Silas relationship. We are harnessed together since we are both officers of Global Harvest Ministries. We live in the same city, we work in the same facility, and we frequently travel together and minister at the same events. However, we also take pains to be sure that neither one of us *controls* the other. I am not trying to make Chuck over into my image, and he is not trying to make me over into his image. The fact that we are vastly different from each other in background and in temperament and in age and in gifts serves to strengthen the relationship. We have entered into a working covenant based on mutual respect and trust. Neither of us is intimidated or awed by the other which allows a mutual openness and vulnerability. The net result is that we continually add value to each other and to each other's ministry.

Transitioning the Global Prayer Movement

Back in Chapter 2, I told the story of how Chuck Pierce spoke the word of the Lord into me that I needed to receive the vision for where the worldwide prayer movement was to go after our decade of praying for the 10/40 Window. It needed to be done quickly. This was one of the most far-reaching decisions I have been called upon to make, and it had to be my decision. It was one of those things that an apostle cannot delegate. I was amazed that, once I asked the Lord, the answer came so quickly and so completely. For the next five years we were to focus on the 40/70 Window, and we were to transition from Operation Queen's Palace to Operation Queen's Domain.

How was I able to design this radical transition so rapidly? Even though such a thing might be exactly what is to be expected from a leader with the gift of apostle, I am convinced that I could not have done it were it not for the supporting ministry of the prophets. Chuck Pierce had heard from the Lord that immediate action was necessary, and he knew how to communicate that to me in a way that would provoke me to take the necessary steps. Three intercessors had heard prophetically that my decision should be to transition to the 40/70 Window quite a while before I inquired of the Lord. The four of them, joined by many others as well, were fervently standing in the gap for me so that when I did inquire of the Lord, He would be able to reveal His will to me clearly. I love this because it makes my work as an apostle so much easier and enjoyable.

The Five Points of the Apostle-Prophet Cycle

If apostles are properly hitched to prophets, if they have established a covenant relationship, and if they have agreed to pull together in ministry, a repeatable pattern emerges. It is like a cycle with five key points. Let's analyze the dynamics of this cycle point by point:

1.   The Prophet Submits to the Apostle
     When the Bible says that God has appointed first apostles and second prophets (see 1 Cor. 12:28), it is not establishing a hierarchy. It is, however, setting forth a procedural relationship. It is like the relationship that a baseball pitcher and catcher have. The catcher calls the pitch, but the pitcher actually throws the ball. Furthermore, the pitcher can and does overrule the catcher's call when necessary. Neither one is considered to have a higher position than the other in the team's hierarchy. Nevertheless, it is true that when the game is over, the winning pitcher, not the winning catcher, is the individual who goes into the record books.

What is the bottom line? Over the course of a season, it is the *team* that wins the World Series, not an individual pitcher or catcher. In fact, it may not be either a pitcher or a catcher, but a center fielder or a first baseman or whatever, who is declared the season's most valuable player. However, no team wins the World Series unless the pitchers and the catchers understand their mutual roles of interdependence. One of those roles is that the catcher submits to the pitcher.

I will not forget the first time that I spoke on these five points of the apostle-prophet cycle to a group of prophets. When I suggested that prophets begin by submitting to apostles, it seemed like a charge of static electricity swept around the table. Even though everyone maintained an appropriate level of courtesy, I am enough of a communicator to know when my audience is not totally buying into what I am saying.

Naturally, this came up later during the discussion period. Since I am so new at this area of ministry, I do not find myself carrying much of the baggage that veterans, such as those prophets around the table, are carrying. They have been around the block a few times, while I am working on my first trip around. Fortunately, they knew me well enough to understand and excuse my naiveté, and they trusted me enough to let me know why they had problems with the categorical principle that "the prophet submits to the apostle."

I learned that there is a residual, knee-jerk distrust of apostles on the part of some prophets. In the last chapter I quoted Bill Hamon as saying, "Some prophets are getting nervous and concerned about the restoration of apostles and are fearful that they will try to structure them into a restricted realm that God never intended."[1] This discomfort on the part of some prophets can be traced to at least two causes, (1) the Shepherding Movement, and (2) erratic apostles.

The Shepherding Movement

Many prophets (and other Christian leaders as well) are carrying unhealed or partially healed wounds from what is known as the Shepherding Movement or the Discipleship Movement of the 1970s. This movement, led by Bob Mumford and others, attained a good bit of notoriety among the fledgling independent charismatic churches of the day. It advocated forming accountability pyramids in which each individual believer displayed faithfulness to God by agreeing on a covenant relationship of unconditional submission to another believer called a "shepherd." This, among other things, could involve tithing their income to the "shepherd."

Pat Robertson blew the whistle on the Shepherding Movement in an open letter in 1975. After a period of intense controversy, the movement be-

---

1 Bill Hamon, *Apostles, Prophets, and the Coming Moves of God* (Santa Rosa Beach FL: Christian International, 1997), p. 139.

gan to lose force and, for all intents and purposes, it has long since moved off the scene. Even Bob Mumford has apologized and renounced the movement publicly. Still, many of the veteran prophets of today have roots in the independent charismatic movement and some were severely burned directly or indirectly by the Shepherding Movement. It is interesting that Pat Robertson, in his open letter, denounced the Shepherding Movement's use of words like "relationship" and "submission" as cultish.[1]

During the heyday of the Shepherding Movement, I had my hands full trying to work my way out of a cessationist mindset in order to embrace the present day ministry of the Holy Spirit. I was in spiritual elementary school, so to speak. Consequently, I was oblivious to independent charismatics and Shepherding Movements, and I doubt if I could have identified either Bob Mumford or Pat Robertson in those days. However, I now can clearly understand why many who are survivors of the Shepherding Movement would have a serious problem with the use of the word "submission."

Erratic Apostles

The second major reason why some prophets have a difficult time considering submission to apostles

1 Harold D. Hunter, "Shepherding Movement," *Dictionary of Pentecostal and Charismatic Movements*, Stanley M. Burgess and Gary B. McGee, editors (Grand Rapids MI: Zondervan Publishing House, 1988), p. 784.

is that they have tried it, and they have struck out. Even apart from the Shepherding Movement, immature apostles have been known to yield to the temptation of spiritual abuse. Because of the incredible authority that God delegates to apostles, this is a temptation that will never go away. It is Satan's Secret Weapon No. 1 in his attempt to destroy the apostolic movement. Genuine apostles who are filled with the Holy Spirit and who choose to be holy in all of their conduct will not yield to this temptation, and consequently, their authority will be a blessing, not a curse, to their apostolic ministry team and to their followers.

Nevertheless, there have been erratic apostles. Some of them never had the gift of apostle in the first place. Others may have had the spiritual gift, but they have attempted to use it without the fruit of the Spirit. Neither of these will work, and those who have been seduced by such apostles, including some prophets, are to be pitied. I couldn't blame prophets who have been caught in an abusive situation and who have gone through the trauma of breaking out of it if they would say, "Never again!"

Submission Is Biblical

Understanding some of the abuses of submission in the past does not give us a license to throw the baby out with the bath water. The Bible clearly teaches divinely-ordered submission. Ephesians 5:21 speaks of "submitting to one another in the fear of God." This is in the context of the marriage relationship. How is God's order of mutual submission to be worked out in marriage? Wives are to obey their husbands as the Church obeys Christ, and husbands are to love their wives as Christ loves the Church. True, some husbands have abused their wives like some apostles have abused prophets. This has caused some wives to refuse to submit to their husbands and to remove the promise to obey from their marriage vows, but this doesn't work—it sends the divorce rates off the charts, and it pulls the rug out from under the nuclear family. It is a way of throwing the baby out with the bath water.

This, as marriage counselors well know, is rarely *either* the husband's fault *or* the wife's fault. It is most frequently the fault of both because they have not mutually recognized God's appointed order of submitting to one another. The concept of submission is not the root of the difficulty. The root is the failure of the parties involved properly and maturely to submit to each other *in the fear of the Lord.*

Let's apply this biblical principle of submission according to the order of God to apostles and prophets. It will work as it should if prophets first agree to submit themselves to apostles.

2. *God Speaks to the Prophet*
Let me begin this section by quoting my definition of the spiritual gift of prophecy: "The gift of

prophecy is the special ability that God gives to certain members of the body of Christ to receive and communicate an immediate message of God to His people through a divinely anointed utterance."[1]

Some people have a problem understanding the gift of prophecy because of the fact that every believer, not just a few, has the ability to hear from God. Most of us believe that prayer, for example, is two-way. We speak to God in prayer, and He also speaks to us, but the fact of the matter is that some of us, day in and day out, are better at hearing God more often and more accurately than others. Why is this? In some cases it might be our own fault because we don't try hard enough or because we're not filled with the Holy Spirit or because there is some sin in our lives that is blocking our relationship with God.

The Spiritual Gift of Prophecy and the Office of Prophet

This will explain some cases, but in other cases the reason why some hear so clearly from God is because He has chosen to give them the spiritual gift of prophecy. Not everyone has the gift of prophecy. If we did, the whole body would be an eye, and this is impossible (see 1 Cor. 12:17). Only a certain few have the *spiritual gift* of prophecy, while all believers

1 C. Peter Wagner, *Your Spiritual Gifts Can Help Your Church Grow* (Ventura CA: Regal Books, 1979, 1994), p. 229.

have a common role of hearing from God and prophesying from time to time.

Of those who have the gift of prophecy, a certain few come to be recognized by the body of Christ as having the office of prophet. They are those who would be included in the list of Ephesians 4:11: "apostles, prophets, evangelists, pastors, and teachers." It is those with both the *gift* of prophecy and the *office* of prophet who form, along with apostles, the foundation of the church (see Eph. 2:20).

I mentioned previously that there are two ways that apostles receive the revelation from God that translates into a clear vision for where God wants the Church to go. One is that they receive direct revelation and the other is that God gives them the revelation through prophets. It seems that God's Plan A is to use prophets for this purpose. The Bible says, "Surely the Lord God does nothing, unless He reveals His secret to His servants the prophets" (Amos 3:7). God certainly isn't limited by this. He can go to a Plan B in order to accomplish His purpose. But if He does, it is probably not God's best for us.

Before moving on, let's be clear that this No. 2, "God speaks to the prophet," will not work as it should without No. 1, namely that the prophet who hears from God should be submitted to the apostle. If there is no apostle in the equation, we end up with another frustrated prophet. I don't know how many prophets I have heard lamenting, "Why won't anyone listen to me?" I would not question whether these individuals are true prophets or whether they have accurately heard from God. They might rate high in both of the above, but the reason few are listening is most likely that the apostle is not there to set things in order so that someone will listen.

3. *The Prophet Speaks to the Apostle*

Once the prophet hears the message of the hour from God, this message must be delivered to the apostle. The better the apostle and the prophet know each other, and the more experience they have in pulling together in ministry, the easier this becomes. In all cases, however, the prophet needs to exercise mature spiritual discernment in speaking the message to the apostle.

There are at least two ways that the *rhema* word of God can come to a prophet. First, it can be a *nabi* type of prophecy, which, according to Chuck Pierce, can mean "a supernatural message that bubbles up or springs forth."[1] While they would not be restricted to this, I have seen two prophets with whom I am quite closely related, Bill Hamon and Cindy Jacobs, receive and speak out this kind of unpremeditated, "springing forth" type of word on many occasions. This comes so rapidly that spur-of-the-moment discernment must be exercised more by spiritual reflex action than by a careful thought pro-

1 Chuck D. Pierce and Rebecca Wagner Sytsema, *Receiving the Word of the Lord* (Colorado Springs CO: Wagner Publications, 1999), p. 15.

cess. *Nabi* is a risky kind of prophecy, especially when it is spoken to apostles or other leaders whose decisions, presumably guided by the prophecy, can affect the lives and destinies of many people.

The second way in which the word frequently comes is through prophetic intercession. When a prophet has been interceding for an apostle over a period of time, the probability of accuracy in speaking into the life and ministry of that apostle increases proportionately. Furthermore, the process of communicating this kind of word to the apostle allows much more room for mature spiritual discernment. My personal experience with prophets and prophecy has pinpointed two special areas for discernment on the part of the prophet:

What to Tell and What Not to Tell

1. The prophet needs to decide what to tell the apostle and what not to tell. Some words are given to prophetic intercessors just so that they can stand in the gap for the apostle, and the apostle should not even know about it. On many occasions I have had a call from one of our personal intercessors with words to the effect: "Peter, I prayed for you from three to six this morning, and God gave me five incredible revelations about you and your ministry. I am allowed to tell you only two of them, and here they are . . ." I am deeply grateful for this kind of discernment. This intercessor is truly a "prayer shield." In

fact, some of my most powerful personal intercessors communicate with me rarely, if at all.

Timing Can Make All the Difference

2. The second area has to do with timing. The prophet might receive a word which clearly must be communicated to the apostle, but the question is, "When?" For example, the three intercessors who had heard that I was to transition the global prayer movement from the 10/40 Window to the 40/70 Window had communicated that information to each other, but their collective discernment told them that they were not to mention it to me until God had given me the word directly. It was Bobbye Byerly who told me about it in the luncheon meeting when I first announced the 40/70 Window, and I must say that she did not attempt to hide her personal excitement about finally being able to tell me!

Prophets often wish that apostles weren't so slow, but they need to be patient because the timing is very important. I can well imagine that if I hadn't been assigned to hear from God directly about the 40/70 Window, some would have tended to suspect that I could have made the decision by caving into the opinion of some who might have had hidden agendas that they wanted me to support.

To give another example, my number one personal decision in 1999 was to dissolve one of two ministries that I had been heading and to consolidate them into one. Chuck Pierce knew from the beginning of the long process that this is exactly what God wanted me to do. We walked arm-in-arm through the months of transition, and from time to time Chuck would nudge me with a word which would invariably be appropriate. When it was finally over and he told me that he had known all along what was going to happen, I said, with a tinge of rebuke, "Why didn't you tell me sooner? You could have saved us months of grief!" He calmly replied, "Peter, I couldn't tell you because you weren't ready. You would have messed the whole thing up!" This is what I mean by a prophet exercising discernment in timing.

Before we leave this subject, let me just mention in passing that at the point at which the prophet speaks the word of the Lord to the apostle, and the apostle receives it, the apostle is submitted to the prophet. This is a further example of "submitting to one another in the fear of God" (Eph. 5:21).

4. The Apostle Judges, Evaluates, Strategizes, and Executes

Now the burden for serious discernment switches from the prophet to the apostle. Only a foolish apostle would receive and act on every prophetic word sent in their direction. As I have said, I only enter a small percentage of the total number of prophetic words I receive in my *Prophetic Journal*. The percentage is extremely low when it comes to spontaneous *"nabi"* words, even those spoken at highly intense moments in a meeting with laying on of hands, extravagant affirmation by those gathered around and tape recorded. Most of these cases, which are not infrequent, involve what I have called "Paul-Agabus" relationships rather than "Paul-Silas" relationships.

I feel that it is my personal responsibility to judge prophecies that come my way. In many cases I am judging the prophecy as it is given, and half way through I know that the Holy Spirit, who has filled me, is not allowing me to bear witness to it. When, for example, the person speaking declares that I will be consulted by kings and presidents and prime ministers, which occasionally occurs, I rather quickly tune out. If it is God who works in me to *will* and to do His good pleasure (see Phil. 2:13), I know that He hasn't given me any more desire (or "will") to meet politicians than to work in a coal mine the rest of my life. I have learned to be courteous through situations like this. When the person finishes, I say "Thank you. Praise the Lord!," and I accept the cassette tape.

Prophets Should Not Feel Offended

One of the reasons I am saying this is that I want prophets to know that apostles must judge their words and filter out those which do not apply. Prophets should not feel offended by this. It does not necessarily mean that the words filtered out are not accurate. In some cases the timing could be off. It is very important to remember that at this point, the burden for dealing with the word of the Lord is on the apostle, no longer on the prophet. There have been, and there will continue to be, many occasions in which the apostle should have received and acted on a certain prophetic word, but did not. It is the apostle who, in cases like this, is responsible before the Lord for missing it, not the prophet who delivered it.

Once apostles accept words as being valid for the moment, a process of evaluation comes in. Bill Hamon says, "However it may be worded, a personal prophecy will always be *partial, progressive,* and *conditional.*"[1] He bases this on, among other things, 1 Corinthians 13:9, "For we know in part and we prophesy in part." These three factors will enter into the process of evaluation. Apostles are not necessarily expected to do this evaluation in isolation from others. In many cases apostles will enter into a period of consultation with other key players, including prophets, in order to make sure they understand the word.

Evaluating Stock Market Prophecies

As a personal illustration of this, one of the prophets with whom I associate had a word in 1998 that the

---

1 Dr. Bill Hamon, *Prophets and Personal Prophecy* (Shippensburg PA: Destiny Image, 1987), p. 145.

stock market would go down in June and begin to go back up in September. My retirement funds, important to Doris and me in this stage of life, are in a self-directed plan in which I can put them in and out of the stock market with an automated phone call. I had a lot of them in the stock market in 1998, so I took them out in late July and put them back in late September. As a result, I made the equivalent of a generous year's salary.

I evaluated that one pretty well, but in 1999 this same person had a word that the stock market would change on September 18 and move again on October 18. I didn't evaluate that one well because I thought that it meant the market would take a nose dive on October 18, so I stayed out of the market for the rest of the year. In this case, I didn't lose anything, but if I had interpreted the move on October 18 as going up, my retirement funds would be worth a lot more at this writing.

Why do I bring up such a mundane subject? For one thing it is because my action in this case affected no one except Doris and me—no big deal. For another thing it is because I wanted to add that I have heard many other prophecies about finances such as some that the whole world banking system would collapse before the end of the last millennium, and none of them caused me to take any personal action. Why did I act on these? It was because of the "Paul-Silas" type of relationship that had developed with this person over the years.

Setting Things in Order

When the prophecy has been judged and evaluated, it is time for action. This is where an apostle's primary anointing kicks in. Paul wrote to Titus, "I left you in Crete, that you should *set in order* the things that are lacking" (Titus 1:5, emphasis mine). Developing a strategy and executing the plan are what apostles do best. It does not always mean that they keep hands-on control of what happens, although sometimes it is necessary, because at this point there is much room for team-building and delegation.

I don't need to elaborate on this because what apostles do was thoroughly covered in earlier chapters. To summarize, apostles are very pragmatic. They do what it takes to get the job, which they now know is the will of God, done and done well.

5. *The Prophet Submits to the Apostle*

I said in the beginning, that these five points are on a cycle. Therefore, no explanation is needed of this point, because it is the same as point No. 1.

Saturation Humility

A final note in the examination of how apostles are hitched to prophets is the need to recognize the role of humility in a healthy relationship between these top leaders. In the horse pull we have been talking about, it is interesting that the 2,000 lb. horses are submitted to a 180 lb. teamster. Humility is important for triumphant draft animals.

Humility is even more important for apostles and prophets. Those of us who are recognized as apostles and prophets need to know ourselves well enough to be conscious of the fact that we have been "exalted" by God. By this I do not mean that we will necessarily receive more rewards in heaven at the judgment seat of Christ, but I do mean that, here on earth, we have been given much more responsibility than the average believer. We have a higher visibility. Many people whom we don't know feel that they know us well. We are on the platform; they are in the audience. We write the books; they read them. We are household names for those within our apostolic sphere. God has made us the foundation of the Church (see Eph. 2:20). Stating this is not a lack of humility. It is "thinking soberly of ourselves" as we are told to do in Romans 12:3 and striving to live up to the enormous responsibility that it entails.

Jesus said, "Whoever exalts himself will be abased, and he who humbles himself will be exalted" (Mt. 23:12). If we take this statement literally, and I see no reason why we should not, we must conclude, even though we might do so reluctantly, that we are humble. If we were not humble, Jesus Himself says that we would not be exalted. By this I do not mean that we should ever stop striving to be more humble than we are now. I would not deny that the temptation of pride is always lurking just around the corner, and from time to time we can and do fall into that sin, but just as certainly, if we were not characterized, day by day, week by week, by a lifestyle of genuine humility, we would not be authentic apostles and prophets.

Humility is implicit in everything I have said in this chapter, but let me be a bit more explicit. Notice that in this process of being hitched and pulling together, the apostles humble themselves to the prophets. Apostles do not go around proclaiming, "I'm the man of God in charge of this ministry, and if God wants to speak to us, He will speak through me." No. A true apostle will say, "I'm not the only one who hears from God for this ministry." That is humility.

The prophets, in turn, humble themselves before the apostles. They do not try to control the way the apostles interpret and execute the words they have received. This is humility, because many times the prophet "knows" that the apostle is on the wrong track. In the apostle-prophet relationships that have gone sour, the lack of humility on the part of prophets who overstep their boundaries and try to do what the apostles are supposed to do has often been a chief contributing factor. Genuine prophets realize that if the apostle makes a mistake, it is not the prophet's fault.

Apostles and prophets can change the world if they are properly hitched to each other and if they are able to pull together!

12

A Perilous Partnership: Understanding the Relationship between Apostles and Prophets

By Jim C. Laffoon
Prophet/member of the leadership team of Morning Star Ministries,
a worldwide apostolic network of churches and campus
ministries, Torrance, California

W e live in an hour of unprecedented revival and harvest. As the spirit of God moves across the face of the earth, churches are growing exponentially, and the Gospel is radically impacting whole cities. Even in North America and Western Europe, the first embers of revival fire are already burning.

One of the epicenters of this worldwide outpouring has been Latin America. According to some statistics, 25,000 Latin American Christians are being baptized in the power of the Holy Spirit every day.

As this great revival has continued, nation after nation has been shaken.

Yet, despite the magnitude of this incredible harvest, numbers alone will not build a strong church in Latin America. In fact, I am convinced that we will not experience the full reality of Matthew 16:18 until we discover and deploy the gifted people through which Jesus has chosen to build His church:

> *"And I tell you that you are Peter, and on this rock I will build my church, and the gates of hell will not prevail against it."*

These gifts to the Church (gifted individuals) are discussed in Ephesians 4:7–16:

> *But to each one of us grace has been given as Christ apportions it. This is why it says: "When he ascended on high, he led captives in his train and gave gifts to men." What does "he ascended" mean except that he also descended to the lower, earthly regions? He who descended is the very one who ascended higher than all the heavens, in order to fill the whole universe. It was he who gave some to be apostles, some to be prophets, some to be evangelists, and some to be pastors and teachers, to prepare God's people for works of service, so that the body of Christ may be built up until we all reach unity in the faith and in the knowledge of the Son of God and become mature, attaining to the whole measure of the fullness of Christ. Then we will no longer be infants, tossed back and forth by the waves and blown here and there by every wind of teaching and by the*

cunning and craftiness of men in their deceitful schem-
ing. Instead, speaking the truth in love, we will in all
things grow up into him who is the Head, that is, Christ.
From him the whole body, joined and held together by
every supporting ligament, grows and builds itself up
in love, as each part does its work.

Simply stated, when the ministerial gifts of
apostle, prophet, evangelist, teacher and pastor are
deployed in the Church, the results are incredible.
The Church described in this passage is vibrant, mature, strong, and growing.

Although all these gift ministries are vital for
building strong churches, in Ephesians 2:19–20 we
find that two of these ministries in particular play a
critical foundation-laying role:

Consequently, you are no longer foreign and aliens, but
fellow citizens with God's people and members of God's
household, built on the foundation of the apostles and
prophets, with Christ Jesus himself as the chief corner-
stone.

The strategic role played by these two ministries
is also seen in the sequential priority they are given
in 1 Corinthians 12:27–28:

Now you are the body of Christ, and each one of you is
a part of it. And in the church God has appointed first
of all apostles, second prophets, third teachers, then
workers of miracles, also those having gifts of healing,

those able to help others, those with gifts of administration, and those speaking in different kinds of tongues.

Lastly, we find the power of these two ministries illustrated in the Apostle Paul's relationship with Barnabas and Silas, who were both prophets.

Why are these ministry gifts so vital to the health of the Church? First, apostles are not just anointed church planters. They have also received a supernatural ability from God to wisely govern both individual churches and whole groups of churches, depending on the measure and maturity of the gift that is resident in their lives. Apostles are also gifted by God to solve church problems, to recognize rising leaders, to impart apostolic passion and purpose, to pastor the other Ephesians 4:11 ministry gifts, and to lay critical doctrinal and governmental foundations in a local church.

Second, prophets are not simply anointed people who give personal prophecies to individuals. True mature prophets, depending on the measure of the gift they have received, have the supernatural ability to perceive and proclaim the immediate word of the Lord to individuals, churches, cities, and nations. They are anointed by God to discern demonic attacks, to reveal Divine strategies, to recognize callings and gifting, to impart prophetic gifts, and to accurately proclaim through preaching or prophesy what God is saying at that moment to specific churches and individuals.

Yet, as effective as prophets are individually in building the Church, their effectiveness rises exponentially when they are deployed as a team. Whether it was Jesus and John the Baptist or Paul and Silas, this dynamic ministry combination played a critical role in both founding and building the Church of the New Testament. It is no different today! If we are to build strong, lasting, world-changing churches, we must rediscover the secrets of apostolic and prophetic teamwork.

This, then, is the subject before us. How can apostles and prophets effectively work together? In order to be as clear as possible, we will discuss this critical subject by examining the problems faced by apostles and prophets working together. Then, we will consider several illustrations of apostolic/prophetic teams in the New Testament. Finally, we will discuss the principles needed for apostles and prophets to work together effectively.

The Problems

First, when one looks at the body of Christ today, true apostolic/prophetic teamwork is almost nonexistent. Whether it was prophetic words that never came to pass, harsh delivery styles, or revelations that were so esoteric that they were of no practical value, many apostles and other governmental leaders have had bad experiences with prophets. These experiences are also compounded by the fact that many prophets, on a functional level, reject all human authority in spiritual matters. Simply stated, if they believe God has spoken to them, no human can tell them differently. As a prophet myself, I know well the temptation toward a radical form of mysticism that can make a person's spiritual senses the final authority in his life.

On the other hand, many prophets have been badly wounded by well-meaning apostles and pastors. I cannot count the prophetic individuals who have been crushed, under the guise of biblical correction, by a leader who was either threatened by the nature of their gifting or frustrated by their lack of maturity.

Why has a relationship with such divine potential been so perilous? First, like all human relationships, sins such as pride, insecurity, jealousy, ambition, and rebellion have impaired the relationships of these gifted individuals. Without the realities of biblical forgiveness, humility, and submission to authority, apostles and prophets will never be able to relate together, no matter how many books are written and sermons are preached on the subject.

Second, many prophets have modeled their ministries after the Old Testament model of the prophet. I do not know whether they have adopted this model because the Old Testament model of the prophet is more appealing to their ego, or simply because the role of the prophet is more clearly delineated in the Old Testament. Whatever be the case, I have observed two things: (1) Many prophets relate to the Church like Old Testament prophets related to Israel. (2) Many prophets relate to apostles and pastors as their Old Testament counter-parts related to kings. For the purpose of this study, however, we will concentrate on the second of these two observations.

In the Old Testament, prophets functioned independently of both the kings and the priesthood. Except in cases where an older prophet was mentoring them, they were accountable only to God. Although they would treat the godly kings with respect and deference, their relationship with the kings basically involved four aspects. First, at times they were used to anoint/crown the kings. Although they did not normally officially crown the kings, their anointing them with oil was a critical step in the process of coronation.

An example of this can be seen in Samuel's anointing of David (1 Samuel 16:1–13). The Old Testament prophets were also the conscience of the nations as well as of the kings who led them. This aspect of their ministry can be seen in the life of Jeremiah, who served as Judah's national conscience for years, even though both her people and her kings refused to accept the possibility of God judging them through the Babylonians.

The prophets also confronted the kings. Whether it was Elijah's confrontation with Ahab (1 Kings 18:1–19) or Samuel rebuking Saul (1 Samuel 15:12–

31), the prophets of the Old Testament were faithful to confront the Kings of Israel and Judah. Lastly, the prophets brought tremendous consolation to the kings. Even the apostate King Ahab received prophetic encouragement and comfort before the most strategic battle of his life (1 Kings 20:13–30).

Obviously, many of these aspects of the prophet's ministry are still valid today. There are times when a prophet must confront an apostle or a pastor. Furthermore, God does use prophets to discern and reveal apostolic callings in the lives of leaders. Even serving as a conscience for a nation, church, or leader has its place in this hour.

As for prophetic consolation and encouragement, it is always needed. Yet, as a "stand-alone" model, the Old Testament understanding of a prophet is at best incomplete and at its worst, extremely dangerous. In order to understand the problems inherent with the Old Testament model, we must take a few minutes to examine the relationship between apostles and prophets in the New Testament. In order to facilitate this examination, we will study the four pairs of relationships: Jesus and John the Baptist; Paul and Barnabas; Paul and Silas; and Paul and Agabus.

The Illustrations

First, in the relationship of Jesus and John the Baptist, we find a powerful example of an apostolic/

prophetic team. Although all the gifts and ministry of prophecy were operational in Jesus, he is obviously the apostolic founder of Christianity (Hebrews 3:1). As for John, we find in Luke 7:26–27 that he was one of history's most important prophets. John 1:32–37 reveals two critical aspects of their relationship:

> *Then John gave this testimony: "I saw the Spirit come down from heaven as a dove and remain on him. I would not have known him, except that the one who sent me to baptize with water told me, 'The man on whom you see the Spirit come down and remain is he who will baptize with the Holy Spirit.' I have seen and I testify that this is the Son of God." The next day John was there again with two of his disciples. When he was Jesus passing by, he said, "Look, the Lamb of God!" When the two disciples heard him say this, they followed Jesus.*

In verses 32–34, we find that John was used to recognize Jesus. Through his prophetic relationship with the Lord, he was able to look beyond the fact that Jesus was his younger cousin and could discern the hand of the Father on his life. [It is no different with prophets today. I cannot count the times that God has used my prophetic gift to recognize the apostolic calling on a man's life.]

Yet, John's ministry did not stop at simply recognizing the apostolic anointing. In verses 35–37, we find that he was also called to reveal the true identity and anointing of Jesus. This was the primary purpose of John's life. He was called to say to the crowds (the crowds that the anointing drew to his ministry): THIS is the man you need to follow. As a prophet, I have found this is also one of my most critical roles. In the family of churches of which I am a part (Morning Star International), I have been used repeatedly in conferences and churches to show the strategic importance of the apostles on our team to the churches and people they serve and lead. I am convinced that even as John "prepared the way" for Jesus, so prophets today are called to prepare the way for a new generation of apostles to do their work.

Let me illustrate what I mean by "preparing the way." Through the power of the prophetic office, prophets can forge the credibility necessary to speak to the most sensitive areas in the lives of churches and people. For example, many times churches bring me in to speak because they love the supernatural gift of prophecy. What they really need, however, is some practical apostolic wisdom to solve the complex problems they are facing. When I find myself in situations like this, I use the credibility that the gift of God in my life has produced to point them toward the apostolic help they need.

In the relationship between Jesus and John the Baptist, we also find one of the great tests of prophetic ministry. This test is described in John 1:19–20 and 3:26–30:

Now this was John's testimony when the Jews of Jerusalem sent priests and Levites to ask him who he was. He did not fail confess, but confessed freely, "I am not the Christ." They came to John and said to him, "Rabbi, that man who was with you on the other side of the Jordan the one you testified about well, he is baptizing, and everyone is going to him." To this John replied, "A man can receive only what is given him from heaven. You yourselves can testify that I said, 'I am not the Christ but am sent ahead of him.' The bride belongs to the bridegroom. The friend who attends the bridegroom waits and listens for him, and is full of joy when he hears the bridegroom's voice. That joy is mine, and it is now complete. He must become greater; I must become less.

Who are you, John? This question precipitated the defining moment of his life. After all, no greater prophet had ever been born than John. The crowds, drawn by the anointing on his life, were the greatest seen in Israel for centuries. They were even coming into the desert to hear his clarion call to repentance and holiness. Surely, like Elijah, he was the physical embodiment of everything God was doing on the earth. He had be the one who would apostolically plant the kingdom of God on the earth! Yet, he was not the One, and he knew it. With these words he passed his test: "I am not the Christ, but am sent ahead of Him."

This test is still going on today. Although they may not realize it, many prophets are facing the same test that John faced. The anointing of God on their lives is drawing crowds. Everyone wants a personal prophecy or revelation from the lips of a prophet. Whole conferences want to bask in the prophetic phenomenon that surrounds their lives. Even churches are clamoring to come under their prophetic covering.

Independent of all true apostolic government, prophets are either self-proclaimed or revealed by well-meaning friends to be apostles or prophetic-apostles. Although the churches in the network they establish will benefit from the prophetic anointing, they will lack the church planting and governing, nation opening, pioneering power that results from apostolic leadership.

I know this test well. There was a time in my life when I was ready to proclaim that I was an apostle. Churches wanted my help, pastors asked for my covering, and everyone wanted a prophecy. This brief period was the only time in my ministry that I had ever been independent of apostolic authority. I am so thankful today that God spared me from a life of trying to be something he had never called me to be. He united me with a tremendous team of apostles who are committed to planting churches throughout the world.

The next apostolic/prophetic relationship we will discuss is the one between Paul and Barnabas. Although it is obvious that Paul is an apostle, many Christian leaders would contend that Barnabas is also an apostle. Their contention is based on the facts that: (1) Barnabas was sent out on an apostolic mission with Paul from the church in Antioch (Acts 13:1–3), and (2) that he, along with Paul, is referred to as an apostle (Acts 14:4). Although these Christian leaders may well be right in their contention, in my opinion, the primary gift in the life of the Barnabas was either that of a prophet or what Dr. Peter Wagner would call a hyphenated apostle (a prophetic-apostle). Whatever be the case, I believe the office of the prophet was the strongest anointing in the life of Barnabas.

My reasons for this opinion are as follows: first, the apostles changed his name from Joseph to Barnabas (Acts 4:36). The name Barnabas comes from a Chaldean word that means "son of prophecy." I believe his name change was a reflection of the call and anointing the apostles saw on his life. Last, Barnabas was far senior to Paul in the ministry when their relationship began. He was the very man God used both to recognize the apostolic anointing on the life of Paul and to reveal it to the Church of that day (Acts 9:26–30 and 11:25–26). Yet, by the time they left Cyprus (one of the stops on their first apostolic journey), Paul was already in charge of the team.

This leadership transition is reflected in the language of Acts 13. In verse two, the Holy Spirit said, "Set apart Barnabas and Saul for the work to which I have called them." By the time we get to verse thirteen, their team is referred to as "Paul and his companions." Was this clear change in leadership a demotion for Barnabas because of some problem in his life? No, it simply illustrated the fact that apostles have been given more governmental authority than prophets have (1 Corinthians 12:28).

As a prophet, I both recognize and enjoy the fact that God has put my life under apostolic authority. When I think of Rice Brooks, Phil Bonasso and Steve Murrell, the three apostolic men that God used to establish the ministry of which I am a part, my heart is filled with thankfulness for their leadership. These men give me (as the senior prophetic leader in our ministry) all the influence, authority, and opportunities I could ever desire.

Yet, I even have something more than that. I have had the fulfillment of seeing the anointing and fruitfulness (of the ministry God has given me) increase exponentially, because I am ministering in divine concert with apostolically gifted men. In a ministry filled with apostles and evangelists, I don't just prophesy about the coming harvest; I live in the middle of it! Furthermore, I do more than prophesy about church planting and pray it will happen: I have the privilege of ministering in church plants around the world, because I have chosen to walk with the men gifted by God to do the planting! Whether it is Barnabas (or me), let us never forget that all prophets must settle the question of who is in authority.

After his separation with Barnabas, Paul invited Silas to join his ministry team (Acts 15:40). We know from Acts 15:32 that Silas was a prophet. Once again, Paul had been divinely teamed with the prophetic. The rest is history. God used Paul and Silas to open up the whole province of Macedonia!

It is also interesting to note what happened in the province of Macedonia when Silas was not with Paul. Although it is only speculation, I have wondered if one of the reasons for the meager fruit produced by Paul's ministry in the city of Athens (Acts 17:32–34) was the fact that Silas was not with him (Acts 17:14). Was Paul missing the supernatural revelation and insight into the invisible realm that Silas could have provided? As I have already said, all we can really do is speculate.

Although scripture is virtually silent on the subject of workings of apostolic/prophetic teamwork, I have learned from my own experience that the ministry productivity of apostles and prophets increases exponentially when they are teamed together. I believe some of the reasons for this are as follows:

1. When the prophetic revelation of a prophet is combined with the wisdom of an apostle, there is a whole new level of strategic application. In my own life, I have seen the apostles with whom I work receive the wisdom of God to apply, with incredible results, the prophetic revelation I receive.

2. The insights prophets receive into God's strategy and timing for nations, cities, and people are an incredible help to an apostolic church planter.
3. The combination of prophetic anointing and the signs and wonders that can accompany apostolic ministry creates an incredible atmosphere for Kingdom advancement. I am convinced that this potent ministry combination will be one of the keys to completing the Great Commission.

The last apostolic/prophetic relationship we will discuss is the one between Paul and Agabus. Although they were not in an intimate team relationship, God used this respected prophet (Acts 11:27–30) to speak into Paul's life at a critical time in his ministry (Acts 21:10–13):

> *After we had been there a number of days, a prophet named Agabus came down from Judea. Coming over to us, he took Paul's belt, tied his own hands and feet with it and said, "The Holy Spirit says, 'In this way the Jews of Jerusalem will bind the owner of this belt and will hand him over to the Gentiles.'" When we heard this we and the people there pleaded with Paul not to go up to Jerusalem. Then Paul answered, "Why are you weeping and breaking my heart? I am ready not only to be bound, but also to die in Jerusalem for the name of the Lord Jesus."*

From this unique prophetic encounter, we can extract two observations:

1. It is critical that apostles be open to receiving prophetic ministry from proven prophets with whom they are NOT in a team relationship. In fact, at times, a prophet who is not intimately acquainted with a person's life can even speak more accurately, because the word is not affected by his natural knowledge.

2. Through the prophetic gift, prophets can bring apostles revelation that is vital to their ministry. Whether it is a warning, encouragement, or comfort, this aspect of the prophet's ministry cannot be minimized. I never cease to be amazed by the power of God to encourage even the most seasoned apostle through a simple word of prophecy.

The Principles

As we come to the end of this chapter, let me take a moment to lay out what I consider to be some of the guiding principles of relationships between apostles and prophets.

Principle 1—Although there is much to be learned from the Old Testament model of prophets, the pattern of New Testament church life is not prophets as independent ministers, accountable to no one but God.

Principle 2—God has placed the office of the apostle over the office of the prophet (1 Corinthians 12:28). Simply stated, prophets function most effectively when they are under the covering of apostles.

Principle 3—One of the hardest of all relationships to successfully negotiate is the relationship between peers. Even though God has placed apostles in authority over prophets, many times they will also be peers and even intimate friends. When this is the case, mutual respect, humility, and submission to one another are even more critical. Even though apostles lead the ministry team I am a part of, we all hold each other accountable, in love, for our marriages, families, lives, and ministries. Furthermore, they treat every word I share with the utmost respect.

Principle 4—Although God has placed apostles over prophets; prophets have a unique ability to bring strength, encouragement, revelation, and comfort to apostles. Therefore, it is vital that apostles be open to the ministry of the prophet.

Principle 5—The fruitfulness of apostles and prophets can increase exponentially when they are willing to work as a team. Whether it is the revelation provided by the prophet, or the wisdom and governmental grace of the apostle, these ministries have an ability to complement one another that is unique in the kingdom of God.

Before I close this chapter, let me say this. Although the information contained here can be very helpful when it is applied, no relationship between an apostle and a prophet (or even one between a pastor and a person with the gift of prophecy) can experience long-term success without the biblical attitudes described in 1 Corinthians 13:4:

> *Love is patient, love is kind. It does not envy, it does not boast, it is not proud. It is not rude, it is not self-seeking, it is not easily angered, it keeps no record of wrongs. Love does not delight in evil but rejoices with the truth. It always protects, always trusts, always hopes, always perseveres. Love never fails.*

It does not matter if you are the most seasoned apostle or prophet, or the newest leader in your church; if you do not have patience, kindness, forgiveness, the ability to trust, and a lifestyle of humility, long-term ministry teamwork (and deep relationships in general) will be almost impossible for you to maintain. May God build all of these vital characteristics into our lives as we seek to birth apostolic/prophet teams that will shake the nations of the world in our generation!

The Church of the 21st Century

From the book *Supernatural Architecture*, Wagner Publications
By Dr. Stan De Koven

Whenever a dissertation or a major thesis is written, there is normally a chapter included (chapter five in a standard research-oriented dissertation) called "Recommendations for Further Research." It is in this final chapter where the author, who has spent copious amounts of time and energy to justify a hypothesis, now has an opportunity to express what he/she really thinks and feels based upon the research conducted. In essence, this last chapter is very much like my recommendations for further research. It is my hope that this book thus far has not been as dry as most dissertations. But, it is essential that we look to the future of what the Church will hopefully become as we return to biblical roots and begin to apply them within cultural context.

As we come to the end of the 20th century, we begin to focus with great anticipation on the 21st century and all that implies. During this natural time of evaluation and transition, it behooves leaders within the body of Christ to garner the mind of

Christ and reevaluate the direction for the church of the locality. The decisions made and changes wrought will determine, to a great extent, the effectiveness of the Church of Jesus Christ over the next decade or two, should the Lord not return. Thus, with a hope towards being helpful, as well as to provide some apostolic and prophetic foundation for the 21st Century, this last chapter is presented.

To understand where we need to go, it is important to review where we are today. My critique, some would say criticism, of the modern Church needs to be kept within perspective. God is using many varied vehicles to reach the masses for the Lord Jesus Christ. All believers should rejoice in whatever manner a person experiences the saving knowledge of Christ. Just because someone comes to know the Lord through a certain methodology does not mean that it is the best way, or even a necessarily biblical way for us to reach the world for Christ. My perspective on this will become evident as we discuss some of the problem areas found within the modern-day Church, along with some of the corrections necessary to see God's purposes fulfilled.

Initially we will look at some of the dysfunctional components of the Church in the 20th century that hopefully will not be carried into the Church of the 21st century. These include the three schisms presented by Dr. Kirby Clemens at a recent Network for Christian Ministries meeting, along with two others which divide. These five primary "isms" include Syncretism, Sexism, Racism, Denominationalism, and Individualism. Each one is briefly covered here.

Syncretism: a Spiritual Blender

The first issue we will discuss is syncretism.

Syncretism is defined as "to attempt to blend and reconcile, as various philosophies" (Funk and Wagnall's Encyclopedic Dictionary). It speaks of the continuous effort to blend modern cultural trends or native religion with historic Christianity. There is no question that the Gospel must be contextualized to our present generation. However, to contextualize the Gospel does not mean that we must give up the basic tenets of the Gospel, or limit its most important and preeminent tool for reaching the lost—preaching the word of God.

It is an unfortunate reality that many churches have attempted to become so "user-friendly" that they present a watered-down Gospel which is nothing more than a social message of love and caring for the neighbors in their community. Pluralism and humanism have certainly come into the Church, and we must continuously be on guard for such encroachments into the life of the Church that Christ established. The historical foundations for the Church must be recovered. Some of these foundational principles will be discussed in the next section. We must recognize that contextualization or

even cultural adaptation and syncretism are not syn-
onymous terms.

To syncretize the Gospel means to accept and
accommodate aspects of culture to more easily win
people to our belief system of Christianity. The methodology of assimilating aspects of culture to make
Christian beliefs more palatable to the populace has
been effectively utilized by the Roman Catholic
Church from the earliest times. However, it is essential that we recover the pure Gospel of Christ, recognizing the need to develop worship services,
programs and evangelistic outreaches that will be
user-friendly in the positive sense. Our presentation
of the Gospel must be presented in relevant and
persuasive ways without compromising the essence
of the message. Christ came to make disciples of the
nations, not converts to a certain religious ethos. A
true conversion experience will eventuate a different
person, with a demonstrable difference seen between
a Christian and being an American or any other
nationality. This problem will have to be addressed
by the emerging leadership of the 21st century.

Sexism: Female leaders?

The second issue to be confronted (at least in
America) is that of sexism.

It is amazing to me how the Church continues
to battle over the usage and placement of women
within the Church. The world, by-and-large, re-

solved this problem many years ago. They recognized that women who have talents and gifts should have every opportunity to express them to the best of their ability. There are very few limits on what a powerful woman of God can accomplish.

Often I am asked the question, "Dr. Stan, can a woman preach?" My response is: "It depends. It depends on if she is called to preach and if she is anointed to do so."

The same answer would be true for a man.

The real question is, "Do women have a place of government within the local church, in terms of the ordained office of elder or pastor?" This debate has gone on for centuries, and most likely will continue to be a controversial topic. It is my hope that the leadership of the 21st century will be willing, through dialogue and prayer, to seek a clear understanding and revelation on the intent of scripture for the place of women in rulership or government.

It has been my experience that there are women who seem to go against the common understanding. That is, they have an incredible ability to lead congregations, even movements, with the highest level of expertise. Whether they are called a bishop, pastor, an apostle or prophet, they carry the ability to function in five-fold ministry authority. Further, to the dismay of many male leaders, they seem to function extremely well.

Are these women mere exceptions, or is this part of the grace of God in the New Testament

Church? Must we necessarily, in the 21st century, place limits on over 50% of the churches' labor force? These questions will need to be resolved by the leadership of the 21st century.

The Racism Scourge

The third concern for 21st century leaders is the insidious scourge of racism.

Unlike the church in most of Europe, the American church continues to struggle with this potentially explosive issue. Sunday morning is the most segregated day of the week. It is an offense to most leaders on the cutting-edge of what God is doing today to talk about a black church, or a white church or an Hispanic church, or an Asian church.

Is Christ divided?

Of course not!

There is only one Church, the Church of Jesus Christ, which is visible here on the earth. As such, the Church should be as multi-cultural as possible. Each local church should be inclusive of every race, creed and color represented in their community. For every nation under the sun has a purpose in the divine mosaic of God.

Racism must be faced head on! If found in our hearts as white Americans, we must confess it and repent. If found in the heart of a person of color, the same response should be given. Beyond words of contrition and conciliatory rhetoric, there must be the fruit of repentance seen in inclusive relationships without limitations.

There is no superior race!

All of us have the same blood flowing through our veins—the blood of the Lord Jesus Christ. The Church must be willing to face the issue of racism, bring reconciliation where required, and begin the process of networking together with the "haves and the have-nots", the powerful and the powerless, all working to fulfill the purposes of God.

Racism is a terrible disease in America. The love of God and the willingness of God's leaders to not just talk about reconciliation, but to actually reconcile, can eradicate this embarrassing condition of the heart.

Denominationalism: Drain or Gain?

The fourth area of concern is denominationalism.

C. Peter Wagner has made a very powerful statement, referred to earlier, that the Church has entered a post-denominational reformation, a New Apostolic Reformation. He recognizes a new type of church emerging that is closer in affinity to the New Testament mode of church life and government. That is, anointed men and women of God have been used by the Lord to establish churches, to train believers, to raise up new works that are then subsequently planting churches throughout their community and around the world.

These new churches do not fit into a standard denominational structure. Denominations generally have a vast hierarchy with layers of administration which must be cared for and nurtured. Instead of the funds and other resources of the local church being used to support denominational structures, they are used for local church growth in the kingdom.

Some of these outreaches, frankly, are self-centered and self-absorbed. Rather than being motivated by the Great Commission to take the Gospel to the nations, many independent churches, which are a part of a New Apostolic movement, are myopic at best. Most, if not all, of their money is kept for their own programs. Their concept of missions is simply to send their pastor on a two-week vacation to another part of the world to preach the Gospel. Though an exciting adventure, this approach leaves no permanent remnant of God's resources from the United States or another Western nation in an emerging Two-Thirds country. Again, denominationalism and its stranglehold upon the resources of God's people must be dealt with in the 21st century as new apostolic networks begin to grow, even within the midst of existing denominations.

Individualism

The fifth issue to be addressed, and perhaps the most insidious problem, or "ism," of our day is that of individualism.

I hear people talk about an independent church, or with great pride state "I am an independent minister." I have difficulty seeing Christ accepting this concept, let alone the Apostle Paul.

What do they mean by independent?

Within American political history, rugged individualism and independence are words that we strongly embrace. We hold them dear as though they were Gospel themselves. The reality is, when Christ died for us, He died for our entire community. When we received Christ, we joined a greater community called the body of Christ, expressed in and through local congregations around the world. Each congregation is to be individually governed by leadership within that local church, normally pastors, elders and deacons. In addition, each local church must be somehow connected to a larger body within their locality. This later connectedness is called "the church of the city" or the "church of the locality."

The City Church

Colin Dye, in his book, *Building a City Church* (Kings Way Publication, Dove Well Publication, Kensington Park Road, London, WII3BY, 1993), has stated that there are three elements to a city church:

1. A city church is organized into smaller, fully-functioning, self-contained and integral units. In common understanding, these would be

called congregations with appropriate pastoral leadership.

2. These smaller units of the city church are recognizable as part of a larger whole. That is, they all fit together for greater purposes.

3. All Christians move and act together as a body to reach the city, warring against dogmatics or personal interpretations of scripture which divide and tend to conquer.

The city church is truly an apostolic church. It has a foundation established by its leadership that includes conversion from sin and repentance from dead works and iniquity. It has faith established in the heart, baptism in all of its dimensions, and all the basic understandings of the Word of God that need to be taught or imparted into the lives of believers. The individual church is often disconnected from the greater body of Christ, which means it will lose its power and effectiveness due to being disconnected from the larger power source of the church of the city.

God is calling men and women around the world to develop this greater concept of a city church, a model of which is presented in the appendix of this book. A city church cares for, networks with, and develops programs and strategies for the greater body of Christ, to reach their local community for the Lord. Further, it is a dynamic unit, working together to plant churches, establish missions and support existing works around the world.

In the 21st century, it is vital that the leadership of the body of Christ face and deal with the isms of the Church. We must prepare ourselves, our hearts, our minds and our spirits for the work that God has intended for us to do, which is to win the nations and disciple them to Christ.

The Apostolic Family: The Church as the Family of God

It was the Apostle Paul who first developed the metaphorical teaching calling the Church a family. If we are going to understand the Church of the 20th century and prepare the Church for the 21st, we must view the Church as a very large, extended family.

According to Scripture, Christ is the head of the Church. The Holy Spirit is the one empowering and administrating the Church on the earth. The Father is the ultimate overseer of all things and all creation. If we are going to understand what is happening within the Church, we must be willing to conduct an analysis of the state of the family of God as it exists today. A diagnosis must be made, not a clinical diagnosis, but a differential or descriptive one, providing a picture of where the Church is and what things need to change.

We must develop a treatment plan for the restoration of the Church. As most leaders will clearly agree, though the Church is still the most wonderful and precious instrument of the grace of God here on the earth, it is nonetheless dysfunctional in many ways.

The Church needs healing and restoration.

God is calling on the five-fold ministry, especially apostles and prophets, to emerge and begin the work of setting again the proper foundation, of bringing correction as necessary to the Church, the body of Christ.

Finally, we need a realistic prognosis for the future. We know that ultimately the Lord is building His church, a Church without spot or wrinkle. He has birthed a glorious Church, a bride prepared for His coming.

As we look at the Church, what things can be readily seen?

On a positive note, we see the Church growing at a faster rate now than ever before in history. There are more people being saved, sanctified and filled with the Holy Spirit today than at any other time, on either a per capita or a percentage basis, since the dawn of the Church age. We live in very exciting times. The focus of much of this evangelism is in the Two-Thirds world. Very little true growth is occurring in Europe, North America, Australia, or the other more "civilized" nations of the world. Where revival fires burn brightest, where people are being saved and churches are being planted, is in the Two-Thirds world. Africa is no longer the Dark Continent, but is filled with the light and life of God. African churches are sending out numerous, self-supported missionaries to the nations. South America has had an incredible revival. Many South Americans are now missionaries to North America and other parts of the world. The same phenomenon seems to be happening in Eastern Europe and in certain parts of Asia.

Glory and honor to the Lord should be given for these wonderful things. However, our concern must be for the continuation of a revival which can only come through discipleship, training and strategic planning. The truth is that the vast majority of the resources that are desperately needed to disciple the nations and to bring them into conformity with the will and purpose of God are maintained within western nations. Churches throughout the United States, Canada, Australia and the United Kingdom have, by and large. focused their attention on themselves. It is exciting to see renewal, along with the positive results, for people hungry for God. Many have received restoration and healing.

Unfortunately, so much of the recent "times of refreshing" have resulted in immature and self-centered responses. "Give me more, Lord" is one of the phrases frequently heard, a far cry from the revivals of the past where the focus was on our responsibilities in the Gospel rather than our personal needs. To the people who are saying, "Lord, give me more," I would ask, "What about your neighbor? What about the nations?"

God's mandate for the Church will not be fulfilled through a consumption orientation. The Word of God states that Christians have already received all blessings in Christ. Our personal blessing is secondary. It is the blessing of the nations and the reaching of the lost that is our (and God's) primary concern.

In the western church and many para-church movements, an incredible waste of resources is evident. It grieves my heart to see hundreds of thousands, even millions of dollars raised through Christian media events, such as through television, radio and even local church congregations, with a primary purpose of perpetuating that organization. They say, "I come to you today on TV Broadcast XYZ, and I am asking you for money so that I can come again to you tomorrow on TV program XYZ. Tomorrow I will come to you and plead, cajole (some even manipulate) for the same thing, so I can come again the next day and do it all again." This cycle of fundraising for the sake of fundraising may not be the motivation of the heart of those involved, but it certainly detracts from the primary purpose of Christ.

In reality, most churches are not having primary growth, that is, growth that comes through evangelism. True evangelistic outreach results in new converts being added to the church, and would no

doubt lead to the building of buildings or the finding of additional resources. However, most churches
that are growing do so through transfer growth,
which means luring people from one church to your
church. This growth is attracted by various means,
including styles of worship that "tickle the fancy"
of the western populace, or by providing unique
programs that will meet the "felt needs" of the community.

I certainly have no problem with meeting the
felt needs of people, but I am more concerned about
meeting the real needs. These needs are the spiritual,
social, even physical needs of the communities that
we live in, which should by all means be addressed
where possible. However, to address the real human
needs of a community will take more than an individualistic approach. It will not happen through various media methods, although we thank God for the
good some of them do. True and lasting change for
a community will come as a result of a concerted
and sustained effort under the authority of apostolic
and prophetic men and women, working in concert
for the greater purposes of God. Merely providing
the best entertainment for the community during
Christmas or Easter will not build Jesus' Church,
though it may indeed attract a crowd. Hopefully the
Church of the 21st century will want more than the
froth and bubble of experience or crowds at the ex-
pense of the witness of Christ.

As we diagnose the Church, we must acknowledge that there are leaders with a primary orientation toward their own self-promotion, "taking care of number one." Obviously and thankfully, they are a minority. The vast majority of five-fold ministry leaders and elders within local churches have one thing in mind: to see Jesus exalted. They are doing their best to bring people to Christ and glory to Him. It is unfortunate that those who are skirting standard methods of evangelism or doing sensational activities for the sake of activity are often brought to the forefront, presented as examples of true Christianity.

I believe that in the 21st century we will not see a revival of superstars or of the great healing evangelists, although healing, miracles, etc., will be vital in reaching the lost for Christ. Miracle evangelism is part of the supernatural church. The future Church will be lead by no-names that carry His name, empowered by the Holy Spirit, equipped by His ambassadors, released into their giftings for the cause of the kingdom.

What then is the prognosis for the future?

My prognosis is positive.

Yes, there are major problems within the Church that must be addressed. We need to find ways to redistribute the wealth from western nations to the world in need. We must find or develop programs and services that will equip God's people for full and effective ministry. This equipping is not to merely teach them how to give their tithes and offerings and live a comfortable, prosperous lifestyle. The equipping needed will, by design, prepare God's people to become everything that He intended for them to be. The laity must be released into effective service to win the world for Christ in our generation.

Further, we must see the emergence of true prophetic and apostolic ministry. Through the prophet, vision will be spoken into the lives of people. The Church in the city will become sensitive to the voice of the Lord, becoming a city of refuge and a shelter for the lost. We need to have the apostolic foundations established. These foundations will include those presented at the church in Jerusalem, where they received apostolic and prophetic instruction, broke bread, fellowshipped in intimate relationships, had praise and worship as earmarks of their lifestyle, with evangelism as their focus (Acts 2:42, 46–47).

In addition to these foundation stones will be the Antioch church dynamics of the five-fold ministry emerging in the city church with special times of intense prayer and fasting to clearly hear a word from God. There will be a willingness to overcome cultural differences, being filled with generosity for the sake of the Gospel, and an understanding of the Great Commission to disciple the nations by sending the very best (Acts 11:19–30; 13:1–4).

Finally, where inadequate doctrine or experience was found, all was set in order. The foundation stones of a healthy family—baptism, the gifts in operation, and teaching for transformation of character and purpose—were emphasized, and the supernatural church was launched (Acts 19:1–20).

Through the apostle, the purposes of the Church can be established. The Church is to be a place where the lost can be won, the broken healed, the misguided set back on course, and where men and women who had little or no purpose can find their place in God's economy. The apostle and prophet must learn to work together with the rest of the five-fold ministry and the Church-at-large as companies effecting communities for good.

Leaders will set appropriate goals for a city, based upon a life of prayer and mutual accountability. Not unity for the sake of unity, but unity for the sake of purpose, establishing proper government within local communities based upon principles of kingdom living. These are essential, as are plans that are birthed in corporate prayer where our work can be lovingly brought into the light of mutual relational accountability. Leaders in the 21st century will no longer be doing their own individualistic thing, but will willingly set aside personal programs for the greater good of the body of Christ.

For the necessary changes to occur, leaders around the world must be willing to face the truth. Each of us has been raised in a form of dysfunctional family. None of us have a perfect model of church family life. All of us have been affected to one extent or another by the craziness of the Church of the 20th century. We should not deny it, but embrace the truth and bring it into the light—not the light of the media, but the light of the word of God—as we gather as God's ambassadors to grapple with our identity and purpose.

It is not too late for us to repent, to seek answers, to have our relational sins forgiven, to determine within our hearts to work together with men and women of like precious faith for the greater purposes of God.

I, for one, am tired of the Church as we have seen it. I am longing for the supernatural church God intended, summarized best in the church in the city of Ephesus. One last time I return to the book of Acts to see the results of the pattern established by the apostle Paul in this great church.

In the 19th chapter of the book of Acts, the apostle Paul finds believers in the city of Ephesus. Once found, he immediately determined their foundation. "How were you saved? Were you baptized in water? Were you baptized in the Holy Spirit? Are you free to operate in the gifts of the Spirit?" Paul made sure he knew what the true needs of these saints were before proceeding, for these things were absolutely vital. He knew that before any real teaching could begin, he must know who they were in Christ. Their experiences in Christ had to be completed with baptisms that would identify them to the Church and fill them with the empowerment of the Holy Spirit, necessary ingredients for effective living.

The apostle Paul dealt with first things first.

He did not set his attention on church growth, on building acquisition, or even on evangelism. He set his heart, as Jesus did, on the equipping of the twelve and the others that would follow after them, to prepare them for ministry. In the 8th verse of chapter 19 we see Paul enter the synagogue and begin to teach about the kingdom of God. The religious leadership, as was common, rejected him, so he established a school of ministry for the city. The school of Tyrannous, likely a rented facility for children or adults, was used to begin the process of teaching disciples, a repeat of previously learned and tested patterns. Paul trained and taught the converts in that city, both Jews and Greeks, all that he had received from Jesus and all he had learned with Barnabas. It was multi-cultural ministry, the only way Paul would have it.

After two years of intense instruction, likely filled with a mixture of the theological and practical growth of the Church began to occur. The result of the teaching ministry, after having laid an appropriate foundation for the disciples, was that extraordinary miracles began to manifest. Deliverance from demonic oppression occurred. People who had debilitating diseases were miraculously healed.

In the ministry of Peter, his mere shadow, when it crossed over someone, would instantaneously and miraculously heal and deliver. How much more extraordinary must have been the miracles through Paul. From these miracles, and from Paul sending out teams comprised of students he had trained into the outlying areas, the gospel of the kingdom reached Asia Minor. People were being saved, churches were being planted, revival fires were lit throughout that region and into regions beyond.

What does God want to do through us in the 21st century?

It will take an Ephesus-type of ministry to produce His supernatural church. It is God's intention to restore back the full functioning of the church of the city, where His purposes for the nations are accomplished. Our purpose is to effectively and completely equip God's people in preparation for the promised revival. God will allow us to choose from a variety of models and methods to complete the task. Each community will need unique approaches, to be discovered by the respective leaders within that given community. However, the primary goal must remain the same; our primary responsibility must flow with the general patterns of scripture. For some communities, a cell-based church model will be best. In others, it may be a mega-church that will get the job done. In other places, standard local churches planted on every street corner throughout the world will be the plan (this is by far the best).

All I really know is this—if we catch the vision of what God intends to do, our hearts and minds will change. Our focus will no longer be on our own programs or ourselves, but we will be intently determined to find and do the will and purpose of God for the expansion of His kingdom in the earth. I long for the 21st century Church to be different than what we've experienced in the 20th. I thank God for every great warrior of the cross of Christ that has come before us and has laid a foundation stone to the church of the city.

Of course, we must take the time to do a painstaking analysis of our lives and ministries, willing to evaluate what has gone before, not throwing the baby out with the bath water, but changing the dirty water where needed. It is time for leaders in the Body of Christ to look towards the 21st century, not settling for church as usual, but seeking instead to settle for nothing less than His supernatural church!

In the 21st century Church, growth and development will occur because of the empowerment of the Holy Spirit through yielded servants of God. The Lord will use for His purposes trained, equipped and empowered laity who will go into the highways and byways and compel men and women to come in, led by apostolic and prophetic teams, discipling the nations until the Lord returns. We are building for the next generation, a generation who will fulfill the mandate for the Church.

"Listen, O my people, to my instruction; Incline your ears to the words of my mouth. I will open my mouth

in a parable; I will utter dark sayings of old, which we have heard and known, and our fathers have told us. We will not conceal them from their children, but tell to the generation to come the praises of the Lord, and His strength and His wondrous works that He has done. For He established a testimony in Jacob, and appointed a law in Israel, which He commanded our fathers, that they should teach them to their children, That the generation to come might know, even the children yet to be born, that they may arise and tell them to their children, That they should put their confidence in God, but keep His commandments, And not be like their fathers, a stubborn and rebellious generation, a generation that did not prepare its heart, and whose spirit was not faithful to God." Psalm 78:1–8 NAS